MW00818309

A Practical Guide to Buying and Raising a Happy, Healthy GOLDEN RETRIEVER PUPPY

Published by Jane Hodges

The author shall not be liable in the event of incidental or consequential damages in connection with, or arising out of, the furnishing, performance, or use of the instructions and suggestions contained in this book.

Second Edition 2023

ISBN: 978-0-6452734-1-0

TABLE OF CONTENTS

INTRODUCTION

Welcome to this new and improved edition of *A Practical Guide to Buying and Raising a Happy, Healthy Golden Retriever Puppy*. I am Jane Hodges, a respected breeder of Golden Retrievers in Australia. Having bred and shown these beautiful dogs for over 30 years under the Camuka prefix, I have advised many families on how to buy and raise their new puppy. Through this book, I want to share my knowledge with as wide an audience as possible, so that all new Golden Retriever owners can enjoy a long and happy relationship with their dog.

Over the past 30 years the popularity of Golden Retrievers has surged, and so have puppy farms and unregistered breeders. I have watched on as more and more puppy problems have emerged, and I have heard some incredibly sad stories. Many people are buying puppies with no prior research and are not provided with the information they need to correctly raise their Golden Retriever puppy.

Seven years ago, I established an online Facebook support group to help people make the right choice on where to purchase and how to raise a new puppy. The Golden Retriever Puppies (Dogs Australia) discussion group is a friendly platform where people can seek advice about puppies from experienced breeders. Today this group has over 14,000 members and is supported by a wonderful team of breeders, trainers, and veterinarians from around Australia.

Jane with Ringo and his daughters, Spice and Shine

I have broad experience in animal health, having worked in the veterinary industry for over 25 years with many different companies, including as a vet nurse. I have also worked as an educator for the Responsible Pet Education program. I have been an active member of the Golden Retriever Club of Victoria for 33 years, and have served on the committee. I was also the Victorian Golden Retriever National Breed Council Representative for many years.

Over the years many people have come to me for advice and suggested I should write a puppy guidebook. A silver lining of the arrival of COVID is that I finally found the time to finish this book – two years after starting! To date, this guide has helped thousands of new puppy parents Australia wide, and many breeders have supported the book by providing it in their puppy packs. Since its publication, I have received many enquiries from international owners and breeders – so this updated edition is for you, without the specific Australian references. I hope you find this puppy guidebook helpful and easy to follow.

HOW TO USE THIS GUIDEBOOK

If you have already purchased your puppy, you may like to bypass the first section of this book. Regardless of where you purchased your puppy, this book is full of helpful advice, from house training and behaviour matters to common health problems – and, of course, how to have lots of fun with your puppy!

In the back of the book, you will find **a puppy diary**, where you can record important information such as weights and dates for vaccination and worming. There is also a **printable puppy socialisation chart.**

A Little Bit of History

The very first Golden Retrievers were bred by Lord Tweedmouth, a Scottish Lord, in the 1860s. He created the breed to retrieve game from marshy land and water on his Guisachan Estate in the Scottish Highlands.

It took nearly half a century for breeders to consistently produce yellow Retriever puppies. In 1908, Lord Harcourt showed his Golden Retrievers at the Kennel Club Show in the United Kingdom, bringing the breed into the public eye. The breed was officially recognised by the Kennel Club in 1913 in the UK and 1925 in the USA. From there, their popularity spread. The breed arrived in Australia in 1914 and was officially registered in 1937, with the arrival of "Grakle of Tone" and "Temeraire" from England.

The breed's popularity worldwide has resulted in the establishment of many State and National breed clubs. Contrary to many opinions, there is only one Golden Retriever breed. They all come from Scotland. There is some variation in looks between countries, especially between North America and the United Kingdom and Europe. However, the breed standards are not dissimilar, with the most important feature being temperament. The Golden Retriever is a medium-large gundog that was bred to retrieve shot waterfowl, such as ducks, and upland game birds like pheasants during hunting at shooting parties.

Golden Retrievers have an instinctive love of water and are easy to train to basic or advanced obedience levels. They are a double-coated breed, with a dense inner coat that provides them with adequate warmth in the outdoors, and an outer coat that lies flat against their bodies and repels water.

The breed is a most popular family pet, and they are prominent in conformation shows for pedigree dogs. Due to their biddable (obedient) and gentle temperament, they are popular as assistance dogs, guide dogs, and search-and-rescue dogs. The breed's friendly temperament means it is very unsuited to be a guard dog, but this temperament has also made them one of the most popular dog breeds worldwide. As a gundog, they do require both physical and mental exercise, which is helped by the fact they love play and are highly trainable. They are not a breed to be left out alone in the backyard, as they like human company.

Essential Golden Retriever Facts

- Country of origin: Scotland
- Temperament: Biddable, friendly, intelligent, energetic, with a natural working ability
- Colour: Any shade of cream to gold
- Weight: Males 32–40 kg, females 25–32 kg
- Lifespan: 12–14 years
- Breed classification: Gundog
- Coat: Double coated, straight or wavy, requiring regular grooming – they do shed a lot of hair!
- Daily exercise needs: 1–2 hours for an adult
- Training: Essential!

The Breed Standard of the Golden Retriever (UK)*

General Appearance: Symmetrical, balanced, active, powerful, level mover; sound with kindly expression.

Characteristics: Biddable, intelligent, and possessing natural working ability. Temperament: Kindly, friendly, and confident.

Head and Skull: Balanced and well chiselled, skull broad without coarseness: well set on neck, muzzle powerful, wide, and deep. Length of foreface approximately equals length from well-defined stop to occiput. Nose preferably black.

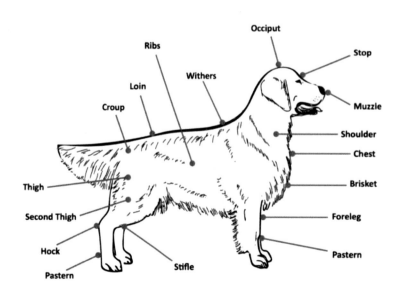

Eyes: Dark brown, set well apart, dark rims.

Ears: Moderate size, set on approximate level with eyes.

Mouth: Jaws strong, with a perfect, regular, and complete scissor bite, i.e. upper teeth closely overlapping lower teeth and set to the jaws.

Neck: Good length, clean and muscular.

Forequarters: Forelegs straight with good bone, shoulders well laid back, long in blade with upper arm of equal length placing legs well under body. Elbows close fitting.

Body: Balanced short coupled, deep through heart. Ribs deep and well sprung. Level top-line.

Hindquarters: Loin and legs strong and muscular, good second thighs, well bent stifles. Hocks well let down, straight when viewed from rear, neither turning in nor out. Cow-hocks highly undesirable.

Feet: Round and cat-like.

Tail: Set on and carried level with back, reaching the hocks, without curl at tip.

Gait/Movement: Powerful with good drive. Straight and true in front and rear. Stride long and free with no sign of hackney action in front.

Coat: Flat or wavy with good feathering, dense water-resisting undercoat.

Colour: Any shade of gold or cream, neither red nor mahogany. A few white hairs on chest only, permissible.

Size: Height at withers: Dogs 56–61 cm (22–24") Bitches 51–56 cm (20–22")

Faults: Any departure from the foregoing points should be considered a fault and the seriousness with which the fault should be regarded should be in exact proportion to its degree. Note: Males should have two apparently normal testicles fully descended into the scrotum.

Note: The Canadian and American breed standards vary slightly from the UK version.

*Transcribed from the UK Kennel Club website: <https://www.thekennelclub.org.uk/breed-standards/gundog/retriever-golden/>

Is a Golden Retriever for Me? Things to Consider

- They are not a breed for the house proud. As well as getting wet and dirty, they do shed a lot of hair at various times of the year. If you have a hair phobia, they may not be for you.
- They are a large, strong breed that requires daily exercise of up to 2 hours. If left alone or under-exercised and not mentally challenged, they can become quite destructive or bark.
- A puppy may not be suitable for apartment living, especially if they do not have outside access, or if you have stairs. They may become very frustrated and destructive living in a confined area.
- They love human company and do not cope with being left alone or outside for long periods. If your plan is to keep your dog in the backyard all day, please do not get a Golden Retriever.
- Many love to dig in the garden, and some are proficient gardeners! If you are a proud gardener or lawn keeper, they may frustrate you with their digging skills.
- Goldens love to swim, and they seem drawn to mud like a magnet, often returning home from walks very wet, muddy, and smelly.
- Goldens are a large breed, and they can be quite boisterous. If you are elderly, physically unstable, or have small children, they can knock you over with their exuberance.
- If you have a senior dog with health or mobility issues, please consider their needs first. A rambunctious puppy that could hurt their old bones or cause them distress may be the last thing they need.
- They require ongoing training, well into adulthood.
- Being a large breed, they are not cheap to feed, and veterinary costs reflect their size.
- Their lifespan is 12–14 years, so they require commitment. Owning a dog will change your lifestyle.
- They require a secure backyard with good fencing and must not be allowed to wander (which they will do if left to their own devices!).
- It is your legal responsibility to register your puppy with your local council and obey local laws.

A beautiful father and son: Thunda and Stormy (L Harrowfield)

FINDING A REPUTABLE BREEDER – Q & A

So, you have decided that a Golden Retriever is the breed for your family. Congratulations! Now the journey to find a puppy starts. Below are some commonly asked questions.

Q. Where do I start looking for a puppy?

I recommend you start by contacting your National Canine Organisation (NCO) (details in Appendix 3) and find your closest Golden Retriever Breed Club. They will usually have a list of breeders (not all breeders will be members, but it is a good place to start). They can provide you with up-to-date breed information. Also visit the specific pedigree dog websites (e.g. in Australia, DogZonline, in the UK Champdogs). Registered breeders have a kennel "prefix" (kennel name), with a specific member number. Breeders must abide by a code of practice (regulations on raising and selling puppies). Every country has their own regulations, which will vary. Some breeders may have also passed additional tests to be called accredited breeders.

If you can, it is a good idea to visit a local dog show or obedience event to meet some breeders and trainers. This always makes a good impression, which may help when it comes time to choose a puppy! You can also contact them via phone or email.

Q. There are puppies for sale on market sites like TradeMe, Pets4Home, and Gumtree that say they are registered. Are these okay?

Reputable pedigree breeders rarely use these online selling platforms, and they usually have a waiting list. These platforms are the home of backyard breeders (BYB) and other non-pedigree registries (many of which have popped up since Covid). Scammers are also common online. "Registered" usually means with their council, or possibly with one of the many new non-pedigree breeding groups.

Your National Canine Organisation is the official pedigree registry. In Australia, this is Dogs Australia (also known as the Australian National Kennel Council or ANKC); in New Zealand it is Dogs New Zealand; in the UK it is the Kennel Club; in the USA it is the American Kennel Club (AKC). To be granted a kennel name (prefix), a breeder may need to pass a test to show their knowledge and agree to adhere to a strict code of ethics.

Q. The breeder said the parents do not have health certificates, but they are healthy. Is that okay?

No, this is not okay. Unless the parents of the puppies have been health screened and hold current health certificates, there is no proof that they are healthy. Reputable Golden Retriever breeders will be able to show you proof of current certificates for the hips, elbows, eyes, and hearts of both parents, and may also provide the results of DNA testing.

Q. A breeder told me their puppies' parents are pedigree, but the puppies will not have papers. Can I trust that they are purebred?

If they have no pedigree papers, there is simply no proof. A pedigree shows you many generations of ancestors, and who the parents are. Without a recognised, certified pedigree, you have no way of knowing whether Mum and Dad are brother and sister, or crossed with some other breed. Who would know? You are buying an unknown.

Q. Some breeders have a waiting list of 6–12 months. Is this normal?

Many breeders may only breed 1–3 times per year, especially if they are showing their dogs as well. Breeding is a big commitment and takes 2–3 months of hard work. New regulations also mean that some breeders have fewer dogs, so are breeding less. Perhaps most importantly, Golden Retriever females should not be bred until they are mature, at 16–18 months of age, and can then be bred only when they come into heat, which happens every 7–10 months. If they do not get pregnant at this time, then the breeder must wait for the next heat. In summary – expect good breeders to have long waiting lists! You should be prepared to be very patient.

Q. Can I visit breeders?

Some breeders will allow you to visit before they have puppies; others will be happy to meet you at a dog show, obedience trial, or park. If you cannot visit a breeder until they have puppies, this may be for security or quarantine reasons, and this is not uncommon. Breeders should allow you to visit once the puppies have been born.

Q. Why does the breeder want to ask me so many questions? This seems like an invasion of privacy.

A breeder who cares about their puppies will ask you many questions. Their puppies are like their children, so expect to be quizzed. A breeder who cares only wants the best home and outcome for their puppies.

Q. Can I specify what colour puppy I want?

Many people have a preference as to the colour of their puppy, but just be aware if you set your heart on one colour you will be more limited. Many litters do have a full colour range, but for most breeders, colour is the last thing on their mind. Temperament, structure, and soundness are more important. Some of the American and working lines are darker in colour, so you may wish to seek out a breeder of these lines. Puppies often start pale and change to their ear colour as they mature.

Q. Is it true that there are two type of Golden Retrievers, English and American?

All Golden Retrievers originate from the same ancestors in Scotland, but over the years different countries have selected for slightly different looks. American Golden Retrievers are often a darker colour, and slightly taller than English or European Retrievers. Their temperament is basically the same. English Golden Retrievers usually have a stronger head, and a very soft, melting expression, with dark, wider-set eyes.

Q. Should I get a boy or a girl?

Both have similar characteristics, including temperament. Both make fantastic family companions. Unless you intend to breed, both should be desexed at 12–18 months of age. The main difference between them is that boys are larger and stronger with a thicker coat, so you will have more hair to vacuum up.

Q. Should I get two puppies so one does not get lonely?

NO! Two is double trouble, and they will bond with each other rather than with you. Training two puppies is awfully hard work and double the time and energy. If you want to have two dogs, wait until the first puppy is 18–24 months old before getting another puppy. Good breeders do not usually sell littermates together.

Q. Is it normal for the breeder to ask for a deposit before the puppies are born or before I can see the puppies?

It is highly recommended you do not pay a deposit (booking or holding fee) until you have visited the breeder in person and seen the puppies (at least by photo or video). Sadly, there have been many cases of people getting scammed and losing deposits. This is an increasing problem. If you do pay a deposit, it should only be a small percentage of the total cost and you should be very clear about what happens if you or the breeder pull out of the agreement. Ask for a written receipt for any payments.

Buying an Older Dog

Sometimes a family may seek an older dog rather than a puppy. An older dog has some advantages; you will avoid the many challenges that come with that first 12 months of puppyhood; they may require less training; and they usually adapt very quickly to a new home.

An older dog may be an ex-breeding dog that is now retired, an unsuccessful show dog, a dog that has failed health testing (e.g. may have a higher hip score than desired for breeding, or a hereditary eye condition), or a dog from a rescue organisation. Rescue dogs may come with their own set of problems, particularly from a behaviour perspective, so be prepared to be thoroughly vetted by the organisation. They are usually incredibly careful about where they rehome rescue dogs, as many have already had a traumatic start to life. Often rescue dogs are castoffs from backyard breeders or puppy farms and need long-term rehabilitation to become happy, healthy Golden Retrievers.

Taking on an older dog instead of a puppy can be extremely rewarding, and generally Golden Retrievers adapt very quickly to any new home that offers them love, cuddles, and companionship.

Just What Do Pedigree Papers Mean?

A pedigree is a legal document. It is essentially a birth certificate for your dog, and proof that they are purebred. Pedigree papers show the family tree of a dog, starting off with the puppy's father ("Sire") and mother ("Dam"), then going further back into its lineage, through at least three and often five or more generations.

A pedigree dog is one whose parents are both the same breed and are members of the official pedigree registry. Every country has a National Canine Organisation with its own pedigree template. In Australia, Dogs Australia (ANKC) is the *only* registry that can issue certified, internationally recognised pedigrees for purebred dogs.

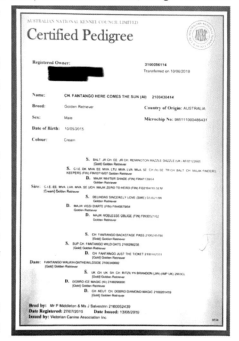

A pedigree paper includes your puppy's unique registered name and number. And you will notice it's quite a big name for such a cute little furball! All pedigreed dogs are named as "Breeder's Prefix, Dog Name", for example, "Bestpuppy Henry Higgins".

The puppy's prefix is like a thoroughbred's stud name or a person's surname. All dogs bred by a particular kennel will have that name first. In Australia, in order to be granted a prefix, a breeder must pass a test to show their knowledge, agree to adhere to a strict code of ethics, and perform breed-specific health tests on all breeding stock. The kennel's prefix can be any name the breeder chooses, within a certain number of characters.

The second part of the name is the name of the individual dog. All dogs with the same prefix must have different names, and a dog's name cannot usually contain someone else's prefix. As the owner you are certainly not bound to this name and can call your dog anything you like as its "call name".

Example of Australian ANKC pedigree

Most countries have only one type of pedigree, but in Australia there are two types. The orange, limited-registration pedigree has restrictions on what is permitted in terms of breeding, showing, and exporting. The "blue main" pedigree paper allows breeding and competing in dog shows and other events for pedigree dogs.

There may be registries other than your National Canine Organisation that offer pedigrees, but these may not be widely recognised. For example, in Australia the Master Dog Breeders Association (MDBA) issues pedigrees, but these are not recognised worldwide.

For every breed of pedigree dog, there is a breed standard (see page 6). This describes the breed in detail, including what a healthy dog of that breed should look like, how it should move, and their character, needs and behaviour.

Pedigree papers are more than just proof that your puppy is purebred. When you look at your pedigree papers, you are not just looking at a piece of paper, but a piece of history – the dogs that lived and bred to ultimately bring you the puppy you are holding today!

The Different Types of Breeders

This or this? You choose.

	Puppy Farmer/Mill	Backyard Breeder (BYB)	Reputable Registered Pedigree Breeder
Motivation for breeding	Profit	Profit, puppies for friends or family	Puppies for themselves or responsible, well-suited owners; or for a particular purpose such as showing or trialling
Choice of breeding stock	What is available	What is available, local dog, or own stud	Pedigree dogs, selected for health, temperament, breed standard
Activities with breeding dogs	None	Usually none	May do conformation showing and /or performance activities
Care of breeding stock	Whatever is cheap, dogs kept in outside pens, moved on when retired.	Same as for any pet. Often inexperienced with breeding and puppy rearing.	Best care of stud dog and breeding stock. Dogs get individual attention, are fed premium diet. Dogs may be rehomed to good homes when retired.
Number of breeding dogs	Many (more than 10)	One or more	Up to 10, depending on region and state regulations
Whelping practices	Females whelp outside, in sheds, often unsupervised. High mortality rate.	Often unsupervised at home. May be outside in shed.	Indoors at home under supervision, with vet on standby 24 hours if required. Puppies spend first weeks inside.
Pre-sale socialisation	Unlikely	With family dogs and family members	Socialisation begins inside, then introduced to many enrichment experiences.
Pre-sale temperament assessment	No	No	Good breeders assess each puppy, and match to suitable owners.
Crossbreeding	Yes, especially "designer" crossbreeds	Possibly	Never (not allowed)
Breeder or breed club member	No	Possibly members of some breeder association	Often members of their state or national Golden Retriever breed club
Health testing of breeding stock	No	Often none, possibly hips	Yes (hips, elbows, eyes, hearts for Golden Retrievers) and DNA testing
Selling practices	Sells year-round to pet shops, in carparks, on market sites or Facebook	Sells occasionally, to pet shops, on market sites or Facebook	Sells occasionally (often 1–3 times per year) via kennel club or breed clubs. Often has a waiting list.
Official pedigree registration	No	Occasionally	All puppies come with recognised pedigree papers, including kennel prefix.
Selection of prospective owners	No	Sometimes.	Careful interviewing via phone, email, or application form.

Visiting Your Breeder

What to expect

When you visit a breeder, they should be welcoming and happy to discuss any question you may have. Expect that you may have to disinfect your shoes and hands before meeting the puppies. You should find alert puppies in a warm, clean environment. Depending on their age, they should have toys and enrichment challenges to help with their development. Puppies should be excited to meet new people and not shy away. (Walk away if you do not find a clean environment and clean, healthy puppies).

Most breeders will have adult dogs inside their house and treat them as part of the family. These dogs should be welcoming. Ask to spend time with the mother, and the father if he is on the property. Often the father is an outside stud dog so may live elsewhere. In that case, ask to see photos.

A good breeder will ask you questions.

You may not be able to handle the puppies if they are young, but if they are over 6 weeks a breeder should encourage you to spend time with them. It is good for the puppies to meet new people. Many breeders will watch you with the puppies to see how you interact. Many breeders will select a puppy for you based on your lifestyle (your age, children, hours of work, experience, etc.). Remember, they know each puppy individually and only want the best for both you and the puppy.

Do not pick a puppy based solely on colour or gender. Temperament and health should always be the priority. Remember, puppies change colour over time. They usually look paler when they are young, then grow to their adult colour. Puppies' ear colour is often darker, and can be a good indicator of what colour they will be as adults.

What to do if you cannot visit your breeder

Sometimes it may not be possible to visit your breeder due to distance, and you may need to arrange for your puppy to be transported to you. This is obviously riskier, as you must trust your breeder to select the right puppy for you. A breeder should ask about your living situation and lifestyle so they can make the right decision. They may request photos of your home and property.

With today's technology it is simple for a breeder to send video clips and photos of puppies, their parents, and their environment, and have live chats with you using Zoom or Facetime.

Key questions to ask the breeder

Are you registered with a National Kennel Council? Are you an accredited breeder or a member of a Golden Retriever Club?	All breeders registered with a kennel council will have a kennel prefix and number. Not all breeders are members of a Golden Retriever club, but most are.
Have the parents of your litter been health screened, and can I see the results?	These should include hip and elbow scores, a current annual clear eye certificate, and a clear heart certificate. DNA tests should also be available on request.
How long have you been breeding Golden Retrievers? Do you offer lifetime support?	You should seek someone who is well known and has a good track record with the breed.

How often is the mother bred?	Usually, females do not have more than four litters in a lifetime.
What happens to females once they are retired from breeding?	Are they kept as part of the family or rehomed in loving home, or do they end up in rescue?
Do you breed other types of dogs?	Try to buy from someone who specialises in Golden Retrievers, rather than someone with multiple breeds.
What is so special about this litter?	Why has the breeder bred this litter? If they say just for the kids or money, walk away. Good breeders go the extra mile to use good breeding stock.
What do you feed your adult dogs?	A reputable breeder will normally feed a premium-quality dog food or mix, and advise you to do the same.
How do you socialise your puppies?	Good breeders will raise puppies in their house until at least 4–5 weeks of age. They will provide toys, activities, enrichment, and a socialisation process.
What veterinary care have the puppies had already?	Ask for evidence of vet checks and vaccinations, microchip details, and dates of worming.
Why have you not asked me any questions?	A good breeder should ask questions about you. If they are only interested in talking about money or when you can take the puppy, walk away.

The Puppy Shopping List – What to Get Ready Before Your Puppy Arrives

❀	Wire crate and/or puppy pen for inside (see *Crate Training Your Puppy*, page 25)	
❀	Soft crate for car travel	
❀	Puppy gate(s) for doorways	
❀	Soft collar, name tag, lead or a harness (a lightweight one to start with)	
❀	Dog bed and bedding ("Vetbed" is great, or a soft washable mat like Conni pads)	
❀	Food and water bowls (stainless steel is best), measuring cup	
❀	Food, as recommended by the breeder (many breeders will give you some food)	
❀	Toys (puppy Kong, Toppl, soft toys, snuffle mat, chew toys)	
❀	Soft brush, comb, puppy shampoo, nail clippers (see *Grooming*, page 52)	
❀	Worming tablets (ask your vet for advice if unsure)	
❀	Puppy school enrolment	
❀	Vet appointment booking (puppy's first appointment)	
❀	Urine odour removal spray; disinfectant, pooper scooper and poo bags; +/- grass toilet mat	
❀	Treat pouch and puppy treats for training	

Puppy Proofing Your Home – Home Hazards

- 🐾 Before you bring your new puppy home, you need to make sure your home and yard are puppy safe. Puppies are bundles of energy with little common sense.
- 🐾 Check fencing and look for holes or broken palings. If you have a pool, make sure the puppy cannot squeeze through the fence.
- 🐾 Block off any stairs or drops. A puppy should not be allowed to climb more than 2–3 stairs when young, as their bones are too soft for drops. Use baby gates inside the house to keep your puppy away from stairs or other unsafe areas. Create a safe area for the puppy, perhaps one or two rooms, preferably with a hard floor to make cleaning easier.
- 🐾 Do a walk around outside looking for dangers, such as poisonous plants (see list in Appendix 1), rubbish, or sharp objects. If you have a large backyard, it is better to fence off a small area until your puppy is older. You can buy good fencing panels in large hardware stores such as Bunnings or online.
- 🐾 If you have a deck or a terraced garden with drops, you may need to fence these off.
- 🐾 Do not underestimate your puppy, as they can be very energetic and determined.
- 🐾 Organise where your puppy is going to sleep (crate, puppy pen, laundry?).

Puppy Preschool

Puppy preschool is an important start to a puppy's early training and socialisation and usually starts at the age of 8–12 weeks. A quality puppy class and trainer can be greatly beneficial for you and your puppy, but equally a poorly planned puppy class can be detrimental. Just because someone says they are a professional does not mean they are a good dog trainer. I suggest you start investigating now. Visit a few puppy schools to see how they work, and ask friends for recommendations. Look for a training school that offers the following:

- 🐾 An experienced, friendly, qualified trainer (ask for qualifications and references)
- 🐾 Plenty of space for a class to spread out (a cramped vet clinic is not ideal)
- 🐾 Good disinfection practices (particularly important since puppies are not fully vaccinated)
- 🐾 No more than 6–8 puppies per class
- 🐾 Only positive training and learning, with 100% rejection of harsh, punitive, or aversive training methods (no yelling, correction chains, slip leads, or rough handling)
- 🐾 No-free-for-all with puppies – only one or two off-lead at a time, carefully matched for size and temperament
- 🐾 Lots of fun and enrichment ideas
- 🐾 Ongoing obedience training after puppy preschool.

At puppy preschool you will make new friends and build a relationship with a professional you can trust to help you through the puppy development phase. Your puppy will get to also meet new playmates. Do book in early before you get your puppy, as puppy preschool is very popular.

Finding a Good Vet

It is a good idea to find a vet before you bring your new baby home, as often this is the first outing you may have with your puppy. A good vet can be hard to find and is worth their weight in gold. They should be someone you trust fully – after all, they may end up with your dog's life in their hands – and they may become a firm friend over the years.

Ask family and friends for recommendations. Visit a few local clinics until you find one where you feel comfortable. The staff should be calm and competent, offer treats, and make the visit a positive experience.

Today there are many large corporate clinics, which can make it hard to form a bond with one specific vet, so ask clinics if they allow clients to see a specific vet. Covid has caused a worldwide vet shortage, so it may be hard to get into popular clinics, and some clinics have wait lists.

Selecting the Right Puppy

Experienced breeders should help select your new puppy. After all, they have spent 8 weeks with the litter so should know individual puppies' temperaments well. It can be rather overwhelming going into a mob of ten 8-week-old puppies!

A good breeder will ask questions about you and your family and lifestyle so they can try to match the most suitable puppy. If you are seeking a puppy for a specific reason, such as showing or obedience, then the breeder will need to carefully match a specific puppy for this role. If you are looking for a therapy or service dog, the breeder may even bring in an experienced assessor from a training organisation to help with puppy selection.

Puppies should be well fed, outgoing, clean, and fluffy. Their eyes should be clear with no discharge or tear staining, ears should be clean, and no fleas should be seen. They should have no signs of diarrhoea, and females should not be wet around the vulva.

Look for a puppy that happily greets you, follows you around, and wants to climb in your lap. If you throw a toy, they should show some interest or maybe even bring it back to you. Drop a set of keys and see who is interested. The breeder should have provided puppies with an array of toys and activities to help their development (tunnels, balls and sand pit, things to climb, people to meet, and lots of new experiences).

Some breeders do temperament testing, which helps them predict what kind of adult dog each puppy is likely to grow into. This allows them to make the best possible match to your lifestyle.

Do not be put off by a smaller puppy. Sometimes the smallest puppy has the best temperament, as they may have had extra care from the breeder. They often turn out to be super adults. However, do not take on a puppy with a known health problem unless you have a vet certificate with all the details, and everything is disclosed by the breeder. Even then, you should speak to a vet yourself to make sure you have a full understanding of what you are getting into before you commit. Know also that a puppy with a known health condition may be difficult to get insurance for. A good breeder will not usually sell a puppy with a health condition, such as a heart murmur. They will hold onto the puppy until it can be checked at an older age and cleared by a vet.

An example of puppy selection

Purebred dog breeders put a lot of time and money into ensuring their puppies are healthy. Breeders often spend many hours studying pedigrees and genetic information to ensure a match is compatible. Careful records are kept with the pedigree of each dog, and serious breeders may even travel interstate or import frozen semen from international stud dogs to ensure the bloodlines stay strong and varied.

Once the litter arrives, experienced breeders (especially those involved in dog sport) assess each puppy's structure very carefully to determine whether the litter meets the standard of quality they are trying to achieve. Was this a successful breeding of these two parents?

Below is an example of a very well-structured 7-week-old puppy.

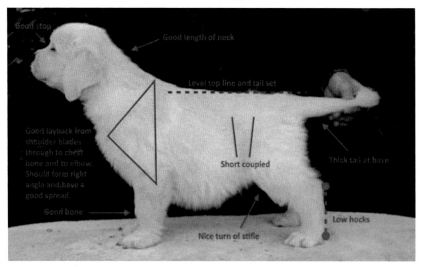

A beautifully balanced 7-week-old puppy (J Salvestrin)

The pictures below show the same puppy at different stages of growth. You can see that he blossomed into a beautiful adult dog.

Left to right: 10 weeks, 3 months, and 2 years of age

BRINGING YOUR NEW PUPPY HOME

Collecting Your Puppy

So the big day has finally arrived! The safest and most secure way to transport your puppy in the car is in a plastic or soft crate. Sitting a puppy on your lap is as dangerous as having an unrestrained child in the car and may be illegal. If you do this, you must have your puppy in an approved harness.

If your puppy is arriving by air, they will come in an airline-approved crate but you will still require your own crate to get them home. A few airlines do allow puppies as carry-on, but normally they travel in a special cargo area.

A soft crate to use in the car is a particularly useful item to have. You can continue to use it when you attend puppy school or take your puppy to the vet. Whenever you are using the car crate, be sure to bring a bowl and water, as your puppy may get thirsty. Also bring some wipes, a towel, and poo bags just in case they vomit or soil in the crate.

When you pick up your puppy, your breeder should provide a **puppy folder**. This should include:

- 🐾 Detailed information on how to raise your puppy
- 🐾 Diet sheet – a list of what your puppy has been eating (type and amount, and information on diet for the next 12 months)
- 🐾 Vaccination record and card

- 🐾 Worming record, including dates worming is due
- 🐾 Microchip transfer papers
- 🐾 Contract of sale and/or a receipt
- 🐾 Pedigree papers (these may be delayed by several weeks)
- 🐾 Copies of the parents' health certificates and pedigree (if these are not included, the breeder should at least let you view them)

Many breeders will also supply a food sample, soft toy, collar, lead, and/or a blanket with mum's scent. Some breeders will also sign you up for 4–6 weeks of free pet insurance.

Puppy Contracts

Many breeders have a breeder contract. This is a legal document that outlines the conditions of sale of your puppy and provides you with a list of terms and conditions (for example – not for export; not for breeding; age of desexing; process if your puppy become unwell, dies, or must be returned to the breeder).

WARNING: Many unregistered breeders will have no sale contract and may not even offer a receipt, so if you do buy a puppy that has health problems, your only recourse is to go back to the breeder. If the breeder refuses to do anything you will need to contact consumer affairs in your state or country. You may need to take your complaint to the small claims tribunal.

We hear some incredibly sad stories. Golden Retriever clubs are often approached by families seeking help after having purchased a puppy with life-threatening health problems, or worse, a puppy that died. Often these puppies have been purchased from an online marketplace, Gumtree, Pets4Home, or Facebook and transported to the family before they have even met the puppy. Sadly, these families usually have little recourse. The breeder just refuses to take their calls or has given a false address.

The First Few Days – Introducing Your New Puppy to Your Home

Those first days with a new puppy can be extremely exciting for everyone, and very tiring for the puppy. But they are critical in getting your puppy to feel safe and sound and confident in their new surroundings. Use these first few days to help your puppy understand that you are their new family and this is their new home.

When you get your puppy home, take them straight outside to where you want them to toilet, and praise them for their effort. This is an area you will want them to get very familiar with! Let them have a wander around and explore a little.

Next, bring the puppy inside and let them wander around the areas of the house that they will be allowed to use. Show them their new sleeping area (this should already be set up). If you have children, make them sit on their bottoms, and do not let them overwhelm the puppy. Let the puppy come to them, and have them offer a treat.

If you have other pets, introduce them slowly and in supervised sessions on neutral territory or outdoors. (See *Puppies and Other Pets*, page 39). Resist the urge to pick up your puppy all the time, no matter how irresistible they are! Let them explore, sniff, and gain confidence.

Of course, you will want to show your new puppy off to all your friends, but I recommend that you delay this for 4–6 days. Wait until your puppy is settled into their new home and comfortable with you. Those first few days are an important bonding time, and can be a bit overwhelming even without the addition of more strangers.

It is quite normal for your puppy to sleep a lot. New owners are often worried about this, but puppies do need a lot of sleep (18–20 hours a day). Growing so fast and adapting to a new home away from their littermates and mum is tiring work!

Enjoy your puppy, make sure their first days with you are fun, and focus on just getting to know each other. After all, this is the start of what will be a 10–14-year relationship.

Post-Puppy Blues

It is common for new owners to feel somewhat overwhelmed and stressed when their new puppy arrives home. Your expectations may be high, and your puppy may not be quite as you expected. Social media can be partly to blame for this – just like your friends aren't always out having the time of their lives, puppies aren't always being cute and adorable! Reality can never quite measure up to the perfection of social media.

Puppies are hard work, they all have their own unique personalities, and they need time to get used to you and their new environment. Your perception of how your puppy "should" behave may be quite different from what you experience. Some puppies do not like to be cuddled; most will cry, bark, and mouth you; and they certainly don't arrive fully toilet trained! Your puppy may also be far more energetic than you expected.

Yes, you can expect plenty of sleepless nights and challenging times, and you may have to sacrifice your morning sleep-ins, nights out with friends, and gym sessions. But remember, it's only for a few months. Once your puppy gets older and into a routine, you can gradually get your life back.

Join a puppy school, and you'll soon learn everyone has similar problems! Just like new human mums, you may find the first few months quite stressful. Do not expect too much from your puppy, and don't be too hard on yourself either. You are both learning, and you will both make mistakes, but none of that will get in the way of your puppy's love for you. This is the start of a beautiful bond that will last 10–14 years. Work on getting into a daily routine, and before you know it, things will start fitting into place. Talking to your breeder and/or other puppy owners can be quite therapeutic when you're struggling, but if you are really not coping, seek the help of a mental health professional.

FEEDING YOUR PUPPY

No topic generates more questions (and sometimes controversy!) than "What should we feed our puppy?" So to simplify things, it's best to discuss this in detail with your breeder before you take your puppy home. There are many different diets that can meet the needs of Golden Retriever puppies, and one breeder's preference may differ from the next. If you have done the groundwork to ensure you select a reputable, trustworthy breeder, then you can trust their recommendations as to diet.

The diet you feed your puppy is extremely important and will have a long-term effect on your puppy's growth and ultimately their conformation (body structure) as an adult. A quality diet will give your puppy the correct balance of protein, carbohydrates, fats, vitamins, and minerals to allow for optimal growth. Golden Retriever puppies are a large breed so, if possible, it's best to purchase a puppy food made specifically for large-breed puppies. And of course, don't forget to always have fresh, clean water available for your puppy.

Puppy Diet Sheet

Your breeder should have provided you with a detailed diet sheet, with a list of the types and amounts of food your puppy has been eating. Ideally it should also include information on what your puppy's diet should be for the next 12 months of their life. Generally, puppies have three meals a day until the age of 12 weeks, then two meals a day until the age of 6–9 months, then one or two meals per day ongoing.

Below is an example of a **typical meal plan for an 8-week-old puppy**.

Breakfast	¾ cup of premium large-breed puppy dry food ½ sachet wet puppy food	+/- dog roll, freeze-dried puppy raw, pre-made raw meat patties (fresh or frozen)
Lunch	¾ cup premium dry food.	+/- cooked egg, fruit, yoghurt, or sardines for interest
Dinner	¾ cup of premium dry food ½ sachet wet puppy food or raw or cooked mince with fruit and veggies	+/- dog roll, freeze-dried puppy raw, pre-made raw meat patties
Supper (bedtime)	Small dog biscuit for in crate (avoid those with artificial colours and flavours)	

Every breeder has their own preferred puppy diet, and above is an example only. By the time your puppy is 12 weeks old, they should be getting two or three meals per day, with about 1 cup of dry food in the morning and another cup at night, plus some extra additions such as some meat, veggies, or sardines. You may also introduce raw meaty bones. Note that the amounts you'll need to feed also depend on the quality of the food you are feeding, and some puppies require more (or less) food. Your breeder should have taken this into account with the recommendations they make.

Feeding Hints

- Do not change a puppy's diet suddenly, as this can cause stomach upsets and diarrhoea. This is especially important in the first few weeks in their new home when they are adjusting to a different routine. Any dietary changes must be made slowly, over a 1–2-week period. (If your vet or a pet shop recommends changing the diet your breeder has advised, please discuss this with your breeder first.)

- A puppy can be fussy with their food for the first week or so while they adjust to their new surroundings. Remember that they were surrounded by their littermates at mealtimes, so had competition. Now that they are on their own, they may be less enthusiastic when eating. If your puppy does not finish their meal after 15 minutes, the remainder should be removed. Do not leave food out for grazing.

- Food is more appealing if served at room temperature, not straight from the refrigerator. Use a clean feeding bowl and feed your puppy at regular times and in the same quiet place (away from children and other pets). Some puppies may need to be tempted initially – you can add a few sardines or tuna from a tin, a bit of canned wet food, or tempting "food toppers". Whatever you decide to add, always introduce it very slowly. And remember, giving too many options can make a fussy dog!

- Always mix food thoroughly, so that your puppy cannot be choosy. If your puppy refuses food, do not offer an alternative, because this can create a fussy eater. To make feeding more interesting you can use a slow bowl or snuffle mat, or a toy such as a Kong wobbler. You could even lay a kibble trail to make feeding fun and give the brain a bit of exercise at the same time!

Food Options

This book does not aim to discuss all the different food options, or get into debates over kibble vs raw feeding. (Though if that's what you're after, there are books and blogs that do this.) Every week a new food or trend seems to come onto the market. Many foods come and go very quickly, and have no feeding trials or research behind them. They simply appeal to people with their flashy marketing and pretty pictures.

I recommend using a food that is backed by science. To this end, I prefer to use foods that are manufactured by the bigger, research-based companies (e.g. Royal Canin, Pro Plan, Eukanuba). At first glance these foods can seem expensive, but bear in mind that high-quality food usually lasts longer, as you are feeding a smaller volume per day than you would with the cheaper brands. Many of the premium brands are not available in the supermarket but can be purchased at pet stores, vet clinics, and online stores, which often have excellent promotions.

But I'll qualify all this by saying once again – your breeder should be your first point of call for any decisions about feeding. And if you decide not to go with a premium brand, a good rule of thumb is to at least check the ingredients – a good-quality food will list meat as the first ingredient, not grain.

Above all, avoid grain-free products, as these diets are very low in taurine and are implicated in a serious heart condition known as dilated cardiomyopathy (DCM). Golden Retrievers are particularly sensitive to low taurine levels.

Below is an example of a **typical meal plan for a 6-month-old puppy.**

Breakfast	1–2 cups of premium large-breed puppy dry food ½ sachet wet puppy food or raw food options	+/- dog roll, fresh meat, chicken necks, chicken frame, pre-made meat patties
Dinner	1–2 cups of premium large-breed puppy dry food ½ sachet wet puppy food or raw meat with veggies. Add 1 omega-3 fish oil capsule	+/- egg, sardines, fruit, vegetables, or yoghurt for variety; dog roll, fresh meat, chicken necks, chicken frame, pre-made meat patties
Supper (bedtime)	Small dog biscuit at bedtime	

Feeding Problems

A common problem is a puppy or dog eating their food too fast. They practically inhale it, leaving their poor owners worried they might choke. Yes, the majority of Golden Retrievers love their food a little too much! A fun way to slow eating down is to use a slow-feed bowl or add water to the dry food. Alternatively, instead of feeding from a bowl, try putting their meal into a Toppl or a Kong wobbler ball, or lay a kibble trail around the back yard. These are mental challenges and will also tire a puppy out. (See more on enrichment toys in *Enrichment Games (Entertainment)*, page 47.)

On the other end of the scale, it's also not uncommon to see a fussy eater, especially over those first few days in their new home. Remember, the more options you give a puppy, the greater the chance of them becoming fussy. Remove any uneaten food after 15 minutes and do not give options. Offer them their next meal at the usual time. A healthy dog will never starve themselves.

Holistic Feeding and Raw Food

Today there are so many different food options, and there has been quite a move towards feeding a more holistic, natural, raw diet. These diets are made up of varieties of meat and bone, vegetables, fruit, berries, bone broth, kefir, and sometimes added antioxidants and vitamins. Many dogs do very well on these diets and seem to thrive, while others don't do so well and may get tummy troubles, so always be prepared to adjust as required. Puppies in particular can be more prone to gut infections or upsets and suffer more severe illness as a result. Only use human-grade raw food, and know the source.

One problem with raw feeding is that vitamins and minerals may not be balanced, so if you choose to feed this way, I suggest you seek the help of an animal nutritionist and/or use pre-made raw diets specifically designed for a growing puppy. Online raw feeding groups can sometimes offer useful information, but as with anything you read online, remember – only qualified animal nutrition experts can give you reliable advice. There are some excellent science-based books on the topic (see Appendix 3).

The wrong balance of nutrients can lead to growth problems, especially in puppies. The best way to ensure the right balance of nutrients is to feed a scientifically proven premium large-breed puppy food. Many breeders recommend you do this until the age of 12–18 months, then switch to a raw diet, or start adding some raw food to the kibble. There are many excellent pre-made raw diets on the market, including meat patties, freeze-dried, cooked or air-dried raw food, as well as raw-food mixes that are designed to be soaked overnight then added to meat to provide a nutritionally complete diet.

If your puppy cannot tolerate a raw diet or if you want to minimise the risk of gut problems, you can try cooking the meat and veg first. This helps with digestion and some dogs tolerate this much better than raw. Cooking food kills bacteria and parasites and makes is easier to digest. I feed my dogs a hybrid diet (combination of quality kibble mixed with a variety of fresh meat, raw meaty bones, fruit and vegetables, yoghurt and kefir). They enjoy this and thrive on it.

Bones

The right kind of bones can help promote a dog's health and wellbeing. Dogs need to chew – it is calming for them, and bones also help keep the teeth and gums in good condition. Feeding raw bones can be a boredom buster for dogs and a great alternative to chewing up household objects.

The best types of bones are not the long, hard, weight-bearing marrow or shin bones, but rather the softer neck, spine, or pelvic bones and those with meat on them. Bones must be large enough that a dog cannot swallow them. Supervise and watch for small pieces breaking off, which can potentially cause gut obstructions (this is not so much of a concern with chicken bones, which are softer and can be chewed up and swallowed). Meaty chuck bones or chicken feet are a good size for puppies. Turkey necks are also popular, as they are large enough that they must be

Raw meaty bones (beef and lamb necks)

chewed. An adult dog can be given a whole or part of a chicken carcass as part of a meal, as chicken bones are very soft. In Australia roo tails are also popular. Bones must never be cooked or smoked, as this can increase the risk of teeth fractures or splintering and therefore gut blockages.

Golden Retriever Puppy Growth Chart

Puppies grow extremely fast in the first 6 months of life, gaining up to about 70% of their final adult weight. During this period of rapid growth, it is especially important that you do not allow your puppy to get overweight. A lean puppy puts much less stress on growing joints than a fat puppy.

Growth rates can vary widely, but the chart below is a useful guide to monitor your puppy's growth rate. Golden Retrievers reach their final, mature adult size at 18–24 months. This is usually about double the weight of the puppy at 16 weeks.

Golden Retriever Estimated Growth Chart (kg)

Based on a chart By Dr Karen Hedberg BVSc

Age (months)	Average weight – male (kg)	Average weight – female (kg)	% Adult weight (approx.)
1	3.0	2.5	10
2	6.5	6.0	22
3	12	9	40
4	16	13	50
5	20	16	60
6	23	19	70
7	25	21	80
8	27	23	85
9	29	25	90
10	30	26	92
11	31	27	95
12 (1 yr)	32	28	97
18	34	29	98
24 (2 yrs)	35	30	98
36 (3 yrs)	36	32	100

HOUSE AND CRATE TRAINING

Toilet Training – Top 12 Tips

This will be your first training task, the moment you bring your new baby home. The good news is that Golden Retriever puppies are usually easy to house train. The speed and success of toilet training depends mainly on one factor – the time and effort *you* are prepared to put in, especially in these early weeks.

Very few 8-week-old puppies can go through the night without needing to wee (and sometimes poo). Their bladders are small. To speed up house training I recommend getting up once in the night to take your puppy out to toilet. Set your alarm for about 2 am. Just pick him up, take him outside, praise the wee, and put him back in his bed (crate). If you do this each night for a month you may end up with a puppy who can go 6–7 hours between toileting.

Follow these easy tips to speed up house training:

- 🐾 Supervise your puppy constantly – this is essential for the first week or two – and watch for the signs (sniffing, circling, whining, squatting).
- 🐾 Always take your puppy outside at the following times: as soon as they wake, after a meal, before they go to bed, and every hour.
- 🐾 Always stick to the same routine: Take your puppy to the same place each time (designate an area not too far from the door), and use the same word, e.g. "Go now" or "Do a wee", to create a strong association.
- 🐾 Give a small treat after puppy has toileted outside.
- 🐾 Share the responsibility (it does not need to be the same person; it just needs to be done).
- 🐾 Use your voice to discipline if you catch them in the act inside ("No! Eh!")
- 🐾 No punishment – accidents happen. Clean up quickly using a urine enzyme cleaner to remove the smell.
- 🐾 If you use puppy pads or a grass tray, do so only for a short time or else puppy will think, "this is the deal and we use this all the time!"
- 🐾 Use a crate. This will make the whole process so much easier, as puppies don't like to soil in their crate and will be more likely to let you know when they need to go.
- 🐾 Set your alarm clock for around 2 am each night to take puppy outside.

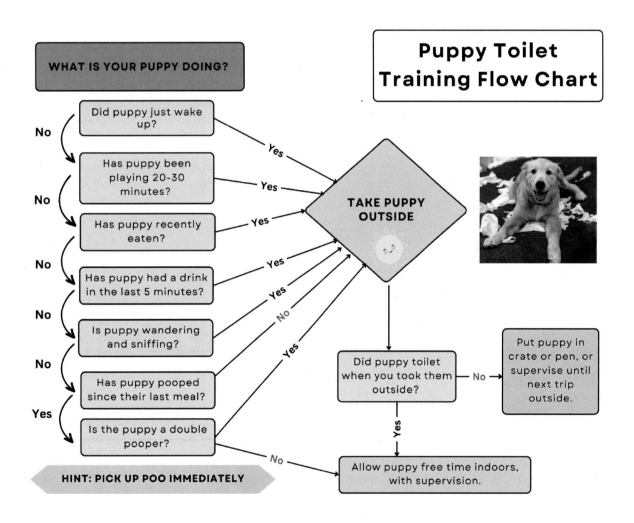

Puppy training flow chart – Based on chart from Flyn Dog Sports

Crate Training Your Puppy

Many breeders and puppy schools recommend you crate train your puppy. This is not cruel; in fact, it is a fantastic training aid that will make life so much easier not just for you but also for your new puppy. Using a crate can alleviate numerous problems, stop other problems from starting, and housebreak a puppy with ease.

What is a crate?

A crate is a portable "kennel" that is used to train a young puppy or safely transport a dog in a plane or car. A crate can be fabric, plastic, or metal. Fabric crates are suitable for short-term use, like in the car, but they can be easily destroyed. Metal/wire crates are more open, collapsible, and chew-proof. A crate is not a prison and should not be used as such. When used correctly and humanely, the dog will treat it like his safe den.

Crates are available from many pet suppliers. I have found eBay to be the cheapest place to buy one. You will need an XL size for a female (38") and an XXL for a male (42"). The collapsible wire crates are best, as the "soft" fabric crates can be chewed or broken out of.

How does crating work?

The key to crate training is to teach your puppy that the crate is where good things happen. Dogs are den animals who like small, safe, cave-like enclosures to crawl into. Most puppies will naturally look for a place to go to sleep that is a tight fit, like under the coffee table. With the crate, you are supplying a perfectly safe environment for your puppy that meets this need for them. I often cover with a blanket or a crate cover to make it even more den-like. The crate is your puppy's haven away from foot traffic and small children; a private bedroom, which they will not soil if they can help it.

Where do I put the crate?

The crate should be in a "people" area, such as the kitchen or family room. There must always be water available in the crate (you can buy clip-on bowls to reduce spillage). The crate should be within easy reach during the day, so that when things get busy and you cannot watch the puppy, the crate is handy. If you need two crates in different parts of the house, get two! Some people have one in their bedroom. Dogs are social animals, so if you lock a puppy away where they cannot see what is going on, you will have a harder time getting them to adjust to a crate. Many people also use a larger pen and place the crate inside the pen, so the puppy can be left for longer periods and has more room.

What do I do now?

- 🐾 Make sure the crate is welcoming, with a nice, snuggly bed and a soft toy.
- 🐾 Introduce puppy to the crate by placing a few treats in the crate or feeding them in the crate with the door open.
- 🐾 Put your puppy in the crate when they are sleepy. If they've already fallen asleep, carefully transfer them into the crate. Close the door.
- 🐾 Once your puppy is starting to get used to the crate, close the door when you feed them in the crate, so they get used to a few minutes of confinement.

- ❀ Provide daily chew sessions in the crate. (We know puppies love to chew!) This will occupy your puppy for a while, and they may fall asleep. Only use yummy chews, so your puppy associates the crate with nice things.
- ❀ Any time you need to put your puppy in the crate, give them something to keep them busy, such as a stuffed Kong toy, lick mat or a chew toy.

The first few nights away from the litter will be hard for your puppy, and they may bark or cry as they are lonely. Make sure they have a soft toy to snuggle with and consider keeping the crate by your bed during this initial period. Your puppy will be much happier if you are nearby.

Set up a routine that works for you and the puppy. Here are some suggestions:

- ❀ Put the puppy in its crate for all day naps. This will make night times easier, as the puppy will get used to being confined.
- ❀ Any time you leave the house, the puppy should be in its crate or pen.
- ❀ The last person to bed takes puppy out to the toilet, then puts them to bed in the crate and closes the door. The puppy should stay in the crate as long as you are asleep.
- ❀ When your puppy needs to toilet overnight (when your alarm goes off or if they are fussing), make it businesslike: take them out without talking, fussing, or playing. After 3 minutes, pop them back in their crate.
- ❀ First thing in the morning, take the puppy out to toilet, following the top 12 tips above.

When the puppy is loose in the house it should be confined to the room you are in with a baby gate. If you cannot be with the puppy, put them in the crate, remembering to always give them something to keep them busy. Most dogs that are crate trained will use the open crate as a resting place.

An ideal crate and pen set-up

The main purpose of the crate is to prevent the dog from doing something wrong. It should be used whenever you cannot watch the puppy (e.g. dinner time or if you are working from home), and as a safe haven away from small children or other pets.

Use your crate as you would a child's playpen to keep the puppy safe when you cannot watch it closely. The results will be amazing!

How long do I use the crate?

The crate can be used for at least a year with a puppy. As the puppy gets older, more freedom can be allowed, but not for hours at a time. Most people make the mistake of allowing the dog too much freedom too soon. When you feel they are trustworthy, you can start leaving them alone for short periods while you are home but not within sight, or while you run to the corner store or post office. If all is fine at home when you return, greet the puppy normally. The crate can then be left for times you need the puppy out of the way, or for the puppy to go to when they want to rest.

Crating dos and don'ts

- ❀ **Do** place the crate in a people area.
- ❀ **Do** remove the collar or harness before putting the dog in the crate.
- ❀ **Do** take your puppy out if they whine or bark because they need to toilet.
- ❀ **Do** put safe chew toys (e.g. Kong) and bedding in the crate. ("Vetbed" is great in crates.)
- ❀ **Do** have water available in the crate at all times (a clip-on bowl is good).

- 🐾 **Do not** crate your puppy too much, as they need play and socialisation.
- 🐾 **Do not** punish your puppy if they soil the crate. Sitting with it is punishment enough! Clean immediately.
- 🐾 **Do not** force a puppy into the crate. Make it so they *want* to enter the crate, e.g. for dinner, chew toys.
- 🐾 **Do not** use the crate as punishment. Remember, it is a fun place.
- 🐾 **Do not** give your crate away. Keep the crate handy even for older dogs; they are great for special situations that require the dog to be confined. Some adult dogs just love to sleep in their crates with the door open.

The Importance of Sleep and Routines

People are often surprised to know that a puppy requires 18–20 hours of sleep per day. You may find your puppy is racing around at 100 miles per hour, then suddenly is flat-out asleep! Sleep is when their bodies grow and develop, including muscles, bones, and the brain. Puppies are not always good at self-regulating, so it is important to establish good routines around feeding and naps. This will enable your puppy to grow and develop into a healthy adult.

Lack of sleep is one of the main causes of unwanted behaviours in puppies. As in children, overtiredness can equal tantrums and poor behaviour. In a puppy this can result in the evening "crazies", with excessive mouthing and biting, and even humping. As well as being important for growth, you will also find that a well-rested puppy is easier to train.

Try to get into a regular daily routine. If you usually go for a run or to the gym, go ahead and do this, but keep it to an hour or so at first to help get puppy used to these alone times. Once they get used to this, you can gradually start going out for longer amounts of time. If you are using the crate, pop your puppy in here while you go out or are busy so they can have a nap. Many people use a home camera to check in on their puppy when they are out.

Hopefully you will have time off work, so you can settle your puppy in over a few weeks. The strongest bonding period is between 8–12 weeks, so this time is crucial for a puppy. Every moment with them is time well spent.

Dog beds and bedding

Breeders often get asked what the best bedding is, and we recommend chewproof beds. Many breeders use a product called "Vetbed". This is a thick, fluffy polyester mat that can be washed and dried very quickly. It keeps dogs warm in winter and is extremely comfortable. It is an excellent product to put on top of beds, in crates, in the car, or on the floor. There are so many different types of dog beds available, everyone has their own favourite, and

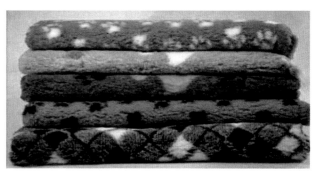

it is likely that your puppy may have several different beds in his first few years. Some dogs take great pleasure in destroying their beds!

The Kuranda dog bed is the toughest bed on the market. It is plastic or metal framed and cannot be chewed. They are expensive but virtually indestructible – they seem to last forever and can be found worldwide. You can buy soft toppers for them.

Pet Insurance

As with our own health insurance, pet insurance has so many options and variables. It also seems to have more and more exclusions. Your breeder may have signed you up for 4–6 weeks' free insurance with a particular company. This is an excellent offer, but it is well worth comparing different policies in detail rather than just continuing with the one you've been signed up for. In some countries pet insurance is the norm; in others it is the exception. Insurance for the first few years of your puppy's life may be a good investment and is highly recommended. The premium will increase as your pet gets older.

So… Should you get pet insurance? Consider these factors:

- Many clinics do not offer an after-hours service, so if your pet gets sick outside of daylight hours you must go to an after-hours emergency centre. These clinics have very high overheads, so veterinary bills can be very costly. If you need to use one of these clinics, insurance will be worthwhile, especially if you cannot afford a large vet bill.
- Many serious veterinary cases get referred to a specialist vet, where the fees are much higher.
- Compare insurance policies carefully, as there is a huge variation between companies' premiums, inclusions and exclusions. Always have insurance that covers hereditary conditions, intestinal obstruction, and cruciate disease. You will need medium- or top-level cover.
- Remember, pre-existing conditions are not covered, so it is best to take out insurance as soon as you get your puppy.
- Some owners decide to open a special bank account for vet bills and pay into this monthly, instead of taking out insurance.
- The most important factor to consider is: Are you able to pay a large, unexpected vet bill if your pet gets sick? If the answer is no, you should take out insurance.

Vaccination

Before I explain why dogs need vaccinations, it's useful to describe how a vaccine works. When a dog is born, it is not immune to any diseases. It gradually builds immunity through exposure to various "pathogens" – infectious bacteria or viruses. When the body encounters a pathogen, it responds by creating special proteins called antibodies, which help fight off the infection. Afterwards, these antibodies remain ready to fight off that same infection if the body ever encounters it again.

Vaccines imitate this process without actually requiring the body to become infected with a disease. They usually contain an inactivated version of a pathogen, which "tricks" the body into thinking it's been infected when it hasn't. The immune system is triggered to fight, which creates those protective antibodies that provide immunity to the disease.

Now, let's take a look at the diseases we routinely vaccinate against.

Infectious canine diseases

The "core three" diseases that we vaccinate for are canine distemper, hepatitis, and parvovirus; in many countries, rabies can be added to that list. These are all viral diseases that, in the years before vaccines were available, routinely caused death in dogs, with puppies and young dogs most at risk. Canine parvovirus is the most common. It first appeared in the 1970s, resulting in thousands of deaths. Regular outbreaks are still common in areas where there are unvaccinated dogs, often in warmer months. Thankfully, because vaccination is common practice today, distemper and hepatitis have become rare canine diseases. In some countries, vaccination against leptospirosis and Lyme disease is also required.

Vaccination schedule

Puppies require three **C3 (parvovirus, distemper, and hepatitis)** vaccines at 4-week intervals. They usually receive the first vaccine at **6–8 weeks** of age, the second at **10–12 weeks**, and the third at **14–16 weeks**. (This may vary depending on the specific vaccine, vet, and country.) While a single vaccine generates a small immune response, to generate strong, lasting immunity, multiple doses are required. Usually two doses would be enough, but in puppies a third dose is necessary because antibodies from the mother's milk can interfere with the immune system's response to the first vaccine.

Puppies should also receive two **kennel cough (Bordetella and Parainfluenza)** vaccinations at **10–12 weeks** and **14–16 weeks**. (These are given in combination with the C3 vaccines, and the combination is referred to as **C5**.) This vaccine helps protect against the more severe strains of canine cough but, much like the human flu vaccine, does not protect against all strains. The vaccine is available in injectable, intranasal, and oral formulations. The latter two are considered more effective.

After the initial vaccination course, regular booster vaccinations are recommended to ensure continued protection against these diseases. In adult dogs, C3 vaccination is now available on a three-yearly schedule, though different vets may use slightly different vaccines and therefore have different vaccination schedules. If your dog is going into kennels or mixing with other dogs, kennel cough vaccination should be given annually, and is required before using boarding kennels or doggie daycare. Regardless of vaccination schedule, an annual checkup is essential to maintain your dog's health.

Titre testing

A titre test is a blood test that measures the level of immune system proteins called antibodies. As discussed above, when your dog gets a vaccination, their immune system responds by producing antibodies which the body can use to fight off future infections. If titre testing shows that your dog's antibody levels are high enough, this indicates that they are immune to the disease in question and do not need a booster vaccination at this time. (This does not mean they will always be immune, as immunity wanes over time.) Titre testing is becoming more popular and may be considered for older dogs, but for most dogs the simplest approach is to simply follow the annual booster vaccination schedule. Titre testing is being offered by some veterinary clinics for adult dogs that have had all their puppy vaccinations.

Worming

Worms are among the most common parasites of cats and dogs and can cause serious health problems. Many different types of worms can affect dogs, including roundworm, hookworm, whipworm, tapeworm, heartworm, and lungworm. As well as worms, puppies can occasionally be infected by another type of pathogen known as "protozoa" (Coccidia, Giardia, and Cryptosporidium). Protozoal conditions require veterinary treatment and can be challenging to treat.

Most of us worm our pets because we want to save them from any discomfort, but it is also essential in order to reduce our own risk. Some of the parasites that affect our dogs can also infect you and your family.

Roundworms are one of the most common intestinal worms and commonly affect puppies. They live in the small intestines of infected dogs and can be seen in their faeces – long, white, and spaghetti-like. They have a complex life cycle, being passed onto the puppy from the mother. Adult dogs may show no obvious signs, but puppies can be more severely affected, with vomiting, diarrhoea, lethargy, and poor coat condition.

Infected pets pass roundworm eggs out into their faeces, which find their way into the soil and mature to the infective stage. If children accidentally swallow these infective eggs, the larvae can travel in their bodies and cause disease.

Hookworms are another common worm in puppies living in warmer climates (though they can sometimes also be seen in cooler climates). Hookworms are transmitted from mother to puppy, and are more likely in intensive breeding situations. Hookworms cause anaemia (low red blood cell count) and can make puppies very unwell or even be fatal. An infected puppy may require veterinary treatment, as hookworms can cause severe symptoms and be difficult to treat.

All puppies should be wormed **fortnightly from 2–12 weeks** of age, then **monthly until 6 months** of age, then **three-monthly for life**. Thankfully, it is now easy to control worms, heartworm, and fleas all at once using a combination spot-on or chew, most of which are given monthly.

Teething

Puppies start teething at around 12 weeks of age. You may notice a few lost teeth on their bed, but often you may just see some blood on their mouth or on a toy. Teething continues until 6 months, so I highly recommend you offer your puppy things to chew to help with the changing of teeth. Options include a nice raw meaty bone, such as a chuck bone (avoid long shin bones), synthetic flavoured chew bones, bully sticks, rubber chews, and frozen carrots. Avoid any sort of raw hide chew, as these are known to cause intestinal blockages and choking and are often loaded with nasty chemicals.

Golden Retrievers should have a scissor bite, with the top teeth closely overlapping the bottom teeth. It is important you check your puppy's mouth to make sure that the adult teeth are growing correctly. If you are concerned about your puppy's teeth, make an appointment to see your vet.

Desexing

Most people reading this guide will have bought their puppy as a pet, not for breeding. If that's the case, you should plan to have them desexed. This will stop some annoying habits developing, and avoid the inconvenience of dealing with an in-season bitch and the risk of her getting pregnant. In many countries it is also a council requirement and means cheaper registration fees.

Why should I desex my puppy?

Desexing eliminates the risk of testicular cancer in males and uterine cancer or infection (pyometra) in females. These are relatively common conditions in undesexed animals, and can be life threatening. Desexing also reduces the risk of mammary cancer and false pregnancy in females, and drastically reduces the risk of prostatic cancer or hyperplasia (enlargement) in males. Desexing also has benefits in terms of behaviour and may reduce aggression or territorial behaviour among males.

When should I spay or neuter my puppy?

This subject has traditionally generated much debate between breeders, vets, and new owners. However, vets who stay abreast of the latest research will agree that any large-breed dog should ideally not be desexed until they have finished growing and reached maturity – for a Golden Retriever, this means 12–18 months.
Early spay or neuter between 5.5 months and 18 months has shown to increase the risk of hip dysplasia, bone cancer, cruciate ligament tear, bladder infection in females, and spay incontinence. Of most concern to breeders are the increased risk of hip dysplasia and cruciate ligament tears, which are very common.

Spay/Neuter DECREASES the risk of	Early Spay/Neuter INCREASES the risk of
🐾 Testicular cancer 🐾 Mammary cancer (< 10% in a dog over age 10) Pyometra (uterine infection) 🐾 Benign prostate hyperplasia 🐾 False pregnancy 🐾 Male to male aggression, leg lifting in the house	🐾 Musculoskeletal conditions (hip dysplasia, cruciate ligament tear) 🐾 Cancers (prostate cancer, mast cell tumour, haemangiomsarcoma, bladder cancer, lymphoma) 🐾 Urinary incontinence, immature inverted vulva, and bladder infections in females 🐾 Hormonal/skin conditions (hypothyroidism, obesity, unmanageable coat) 🐾 Behaviour problems (fear biting, dog aggression, timidity, sexual behaviours)

(See Appendix 3 for references, page 75.)

A caution about Juvenile Pubic Symphysiodesis (JPS surgery)

If your vet suspects that your puppy may have hip dysplasia, they may recommend hip X-rays under sedation or anaesthesia. The hips will then be assessed for "laxity" (looseness). If the hips do appear loose, your vet may offer "juvenile pubic symphysiodesis" surgery as an early intervention to reduce hip dysplasia. This invasive and expensive surgery must be done when your puppy is less than 20 weeks of age. Most breeders feel that this treatment should not be required if your puppy has come from generations of hip-scored parents. If this procedure is offered by your vet, please discuss it with your breeder first and seek the opinion of a veterinary orthopaedic specialist before you consider going ahead. Do not feel pressured into it by your vet.

Retained testicle (Cryptorchidism)

At birth, the testicles of a male puppy are positioned in the abdomen. Usually, they descend into the scrotum at 7–10 days of age and should be able to be felt in or near the scrotum by 6–12 weeks of age. Cryptorchidism is a condition where one or both testicles have not dropped down by this time. Surgical removal of retained testicles is recommended after 12 months of age, as retained testicles are at increased risk of cancer. Cryptorchidism is heritable, so dogs with retained testicle(s) should not be bred.

Help! My Girl Is in Season!

If you have a female puppy, you can expect her to come into season ("oestrus") at 7–14 months of age. Some girls will go even longer before their first season. You will notice your girl may become a bit sooky, and want more cuddles. Male dogs may also be interested in her. Once her season starts usually you will see blood on her feathering, and her vulva will look swollen (especially mid-season). Some girls will only bleed for 7 days, but others can bleed for up to 21 days. Some girls also have a slight odour.

Every female is different, but in general, standing heat (when the female will let the male mate her) starts 7–10 days after the start of bleeding and lasts for 7–10 days. Your dog must be kept away from male dogs during this time. Male dogs have been known to dig under or climb over extremely high fences to get to an in-season girl, so she needs to be very secure.

Stick to the following advice:

🐾 **To exercise**, avoid other dogs. Drive to a remote location away from other dogs, and keep her on a lead.

🐾 **Keep your backyard and gate securely locked** to ensure she can't escape and male dogs can't reach her. If in doubt, keep her inside. You can also use "bitch spray" to help mask the smell that makes the bitch attractive to male dogs during heat.

🐾 **Segregate any male dogs in your house for at least 28 days** to prevent breeding. This applies even if they are littermates. Some choose to send the male away to friends.

🐾 **Minimise mess** by confining your girl to easy-to-clean floors and using **Hygiene or Bitch Pants**. These help stop furniture and carpets from becoming stained by the discharge. They are made from stretch nylon for easy washing and have adjustable straps. You simply apply a replacement pad inside the pants, just like a sanitary towel. Remember to take the pants off regularly so she can go to the toilet and clean herself.

🐾 **Don't ignore the possibility of accidental breeding!** If you suspect or know that a male dog may have managed to get to your female dog despite your best efforts, see your vet immediately. It is possible to terminate a pregnancy or desex her in the early stages. Your vet will advise you on the best option depending on your circumstances.

If you have no plans to breed from your girl, she can be safely desexed 2 months after her season finishes.

BREEDING YOUR GOLDEN RETRIEVER

Breeding is not something to be taken lightly. It requires commitment, time, a financial investment, and lots of planning. Responsible breeders are members of their National Canine Organisation and breed or dog sports clubs, and are dedicated to doing the best they can for the breed. This might mean spending time showing their dogs or doing dog sports like tracking, obedience, field trials, agility training, and socialising puppies. Their dogs are also registered with a National Canine Organisation, and cannot be bred with unregistered dogs.

Unfortunately, many people just decide to breed their bitch with very little understanding of pedigrees, conformation, temperament, or hereditary problems. They give little thought to the sire and pick the first dog they come across. This is fraught with danger, as there is a risk of hereditary problems if the parents are not health tested, and he may even be closely related.

Responsible breeders breed to improve health, structure, and temperament in every generation. They understand the **breed standard**, only use **health-tested parents**, and seek the best stud dog they can find, which may mean travelling interstate or using frozen semen, not just choosing the dog down the road!

A stud dog should be an outstanding example of the breed. Most good stud dogs are proven in the show ring or other sports, and have been comprehensively health tested. Breeders evaluate their breeding stock and pair them with suitable mates. Normally the bitch is brought to the dog for breeding, or frozen

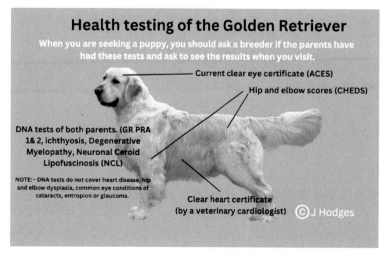

Health testing of the Golden Retriever

When you are seeking a puppy, you should ask a breeder if the parents have had these tests and ask to see the results when you visit.

Current clear eye certificate (ACES)

Hip and elbow scores (CHEDS)

DNA tests of both parents. (GR PRA 1 & 2, ichthyosis, Degenerative Myelopathy, Neuronal Ceroid Lipofuscinosis (NCL)

NOTE:- DNA tests do not cover heart disease, hip and elbow dysplasia, common eye conditions of cataracts, entropion or glaucoma.

Clear heart certificate (by a veterinary cardiologist) ©J Hodges semen may be used, which requires the services of a reproductive vet. The correct breeding time is usually determined by serial progesterone tests to determine the time of ovulation.

I highly recommend that you discuss any breeding plans with your puppy's breeder at the time of purchase, as many puppies are sold on a non-breeding contract. Be honest if you are thinking about breeding.

If you plan to breed with your dog with the breeder's consent, many breeders will support and mentor you through the process. This involves studying the breed, pedigrees, whelping, and raising healthy puppies. It means gathering the equipment required, joining your National Canine Organisation, and learning how you can improve. Learning never ends, and each litter has its own unique challenges.

STOP!
Before breeding, check your puppy is not on a non - breeding contract.

A female dog is pregnant for 63 days. Puppies are born blind and deaf and covered in short fur. They require a warm, regulated environmental temperature and constant care and supervision for the first 3 weeks, as does the mother. Once the puppies are moving around, they will require a secure area to explore, and they can start eating 4–5 meals of solid food per day.

Breeding is not essential for your dog, and will not make them a better dog or change their temperament. Dogs with poor temperaments or hereditary conditions should never be bred.

Breeding "so your children can see the miracle of birth" may in fact upset them. It is a very messy business and often happens in the middle of the night, and an audience is the last thing a whelping mother wants. Puppies do die, as can the mother in rare cases. The last thing a new mum wants is to be upset by noisy, excited children when she has new babies. She needs peace and quiet, and if she doesn't get it she can become very stressed and even protective.

Considerations Before Breeding

Most people have no intention of breeding their dog, but if you are contemplating dog breeding, there are certain questions that you will need to ask yourself before proceeding:

- 🐾 **Is my dog a good example of the breed?** Do they meet the breed standard? Do they have any structural faults, such as an incorrect bite or a less than ideal temperament? No dog that is timid, anxious, or aggressive should be bred. Have they passed all the necessary health testing, such as hip and elbow scoring, eye and heart certification, and DNA testing? Are they registered with a National Canine Organisation?

- 🐾 **Do I have the time to devote to a litter?** The puppies will need constant care and supervision until they are old enough to go to their new homes, at a minimum of 8 weeks of age. Even more intensive care will be required if the mum and/or puppies become unwell. Most breeders take time off work and sleep next to the whelp box for the first 2–3 weeks, with very little sleep. They may use a puppy raising program such as "Puppy Culture", which is very time consuming and can be exhausting. Puppies require 4–5 meals per days when young. Many breeders stay home for the whole 8 weeks because of the risk of carrying in an infection to the puppies.

- 🐾 **Can I afford it?** There are many costs associated with breeding – pre-mating health tests for mum, the stud fee, the whelping set-up (whelping box, puppy pens, dry bedding, heat mat), food for mum and puppies, litter registration, puppy health testing, check-ups, vaccinations and microchipping… the list goes on! Perhaps most importantly, you must be ready to spend thousands if things go south at whelping time, particularly if an emergency Caesarean is required. Another often overlooked and potentially sizable cost is refunds and/or veterinary costs for puppies that die or develop a health problem early in life. In some countries new consumer laws require breeders to guarantee a puppy for up to 3 years.

- 🐾 **Am I prepared for the whelping?** Do I know enough to help the dam during the whelping, if necessary? Am I willing to forgo sleep for 24–48 hours while she is in labour? Do I have a vet on call 24 hours, and am I prepared to travel to an after-hours vet in an emergency?

- 🐾 **Do I have the knowledge to raise a litter correctly?** Can I advise new owners on the various aspects of caring for their puppies, including rearing, diet, training, and health problems? Do I understand how to follow my kennel club code of ethics for breeding?

- 🐾 **Do I have enough room?** Do I have the space to care for and raise a big litter of 10–12 puppies? Sharing your home with a litter of puppies is messy, smelly, and noisy, and they can damage your home and destroy your garden.

- 🐾 **Do I have the emotional strength to deal with things going wrong?** It is not uncommon for puppies to become unwell or even die or be euthanised due to congenital defects.

- 🐾 **Am I prepared to wait to find the right forever homes?** How will I find good homes for these puppies? What will I do if I cannot find good homes for them all? Am I prepared to take care of them all until suitable homes can be found? Responsible breeders carefully evaluate every prospective owner to ensure they are suitable.

- 🐾 **Am I willing to offer the new owners my support?** Can I offer advice and lifetime support to my puppy families? Will I take back or rehome puppies if it becomes necessary? Being a breeder is a lifetime commitment.

Be prepared for sleepless nights and exhausting days. Worry and relief. Happiness, pride, and accomplishment, but also blood, sweat, and tears.

PUPPY EXERCISE & BEHAVIOUR

Puppy Exercise

Most of a puppy's exercise until 18 months of age should consist of lots of free play, exploring, sniffing, and wandering around. If they show signs of tiredness, flop down, or refuse to walk, you should listen and let them rest.

"Sniff and stroll" is a fun way to take your puppy out into your backyard, or if you enjoy the outdoors, take your puppy to a park (once they are fully vaccinated) and let them explore at their own pace and their own discretion, on a long lead.

If you have a larger property, you can lay a kibble trail and let your puppy have fun following this and using their brain. (This should be part of their daily food ration, not on top of it.)

Continuous walking on a lead is forced exercise, which is not good for soft bones. Sniff and stroll is a much better idea, as the puppy can do things at their own pace.

If you have stairs at home, great care needs to be taken. Puppies forced to go up and down stairs are far more likely to have hip problems. The more you can keep them away from the stairs, the better. It is worth investing in a baby gate.

The Golden exercise rule is 1 minute of daily exercise per week of age, e.g. 12 weeks equals 12 minutes of lead walking per day; 20 weeks equals 20 minutes.

Exercise guidelines for puppies

Activity	8–12 weeks	12–16 weeks	4–6 months	6–12 months	12–18 months
Continuous leash walking	2–5 mins	12–16 mins	16–25 mins	20–30 mins	30–40 mins
Sniff and stroll	10–15 mins	15–20 mins	Up to 45 mins	Up to 1 hour	Up to 1 hour
Kibble trail	As long as they like	As long as they like	As long as they like	As long as they like	As long as they like
Running	As much as they like on their own	As much as they like on their own	As much as they like on their own	As much as they like on their own	As much as they like on their own
Jumping, stairs, impact activities	If more than two stairs, carry. A wobble board is okay.	If more than two stairs, carry. Wobble board okay.	Supervise stairs, only allow very low jumps of 10 cm or less.	Take care on stairs.	Take care on stairs.
Swimming	Should wear a life jacket. Wading play on shore is fine.	Should wear a life jacket. Wading play on shore is fine. Swimming okay if they try.	Wading play on shore is fine. Swimming okay if they try.	May still need life jacket. Wading play on shore is fine. Swimming okay if they try.	Okay to free swim if confident. Retrieving in water is good, just watch for tiredness
Chasing	Roll balls and drag toys. Encourage retrieving (5 mins)	Roll balls and drag toys. Encourage retrieving.	Roll balls and drag toys. Encourage retrieving.	Roll balls and drag toys. Encourage retrieving.	Roll balls and drag toys, let puppy retrieve.
Tug toy or flirt pole	Low play, let puppy drag you gently.	Low play, let puppy drag you gently.	Low play, let puppy drag you gently.	Low play, let puppy drag you gently.	Low play, let puppy drag you gently.
Fast turns	No fast turns or sudden stops.	No fast turns or sudden stops.	No fast turns or sudden stops.	Weaving okay if slow.	Weaving okay if slow.
Free play with other dogs	10–15 mins for formal play dates	10–15 mins for formal play dates	Up to 20 mins, can have free access to adults but watch for rough play. Must supervise.	Up to 20 mins, can have free access to adults but watch for rough play.	Up to 30 mins, can have free access to adults but watch for rough play.

Chewing and Chew Toys

Puppies love to chew; they are little organic chewing machines! Remove anything breakable and/or chewable within the puppy's reach. A puppy uses their jaws and mouth in the same way we use our hands – to grab and investigate. Chewing is natural behaviour for a dog. A puppy's adult teeth erupt at 3–7 months of age, and chewing helps the new teeth to emerge. Chewing is not just due to teething.

A puppy does not understand the difference between a rubber Kong toy and the TV remote, or a soft toy and your favourite slipper. Puppy-proof your home by moving anything that they should not chew out

of reach. Pick up your socks, Lego, TV remotes, cables, underwear, and shoes. Do not give your puppy old slippers to chew, or your pup will regard all shoes as fair game! Socks are notorious for causing intestinal obstructions, so teach the kids to pick up after themselves.

Your role is not to stop the chewing. Puppies need to chew for up to 4 hours a day. Your role is to provide "legal" chewing opportunities. Make sure they have a variety of things to chew, including soft toys (no glass or plastic eyes), stuffed Kongs, lick mats, wood toys, and chew bones. Be wary of cheap plastic, rope, or rubber toys with pieces that might break off and be swallowed, and small toys that can be swallowed whole.

Do not use rawhide chews, as these can cause choking and intestinal blockages. A cardboard box, scrunched-up newspaper, or an egg carton with treats inside can make a good toy to destroy (if you don't mind the mess!).

There is no need to scold your puppy for chewing the wrong thing. Just remove it, tell yourself off for being careless, and offer him one of his own chew toys. Use doors and baby gates to keep your puppy in a room where they can be supervised or use your crate if you are too busy to watch for an hour or so.

Hint: You can smear Vicks VapoRub on wooden furniture legs to discourage chewing.

Puppies and Children

The Golden Retriever has a reputation of being exceptionally good with children. However, children and dogs do not automatically start with a wonderful relationship. Parents must be willing to help teach their children acceptable boundaries and rules regarding interaction with a puppy. Management and proper socialisation are the foundation for a safe and fun relationship between children and dogs.

Supervision

Children under 4 should never be left alone with a dog. This is the age group that is most at risk of dog bites and accidents. Any interaction needs to be supervised. Pets and children do not have an innate understanding of how they should behave around each other. A puppy sees a small child as another puppy. Toddlers can accidentally injure or alarm a dog by falling on them, pulling their ears, poking their eyes, or putting their hand in the food bowl when puppy is eating. A startled dog may react impulsively by biting.

All children need to learn respect for their puppy. A puppy must not be teased or intentionally hurt and needs time to themselves. Even the most tolerant dog needs peace and quiet sometimes. Make sure your puppy has a place where they can rest and eat undisturbed. Remember, puppies are babies and need lots of sleep. I highly recommend a crate if you have young children. Children should be taught not to wake a sleeping puppy.

Dogs should be left alone when they are :	Do not allow children to:
🐾 Sleeping 🐾 Eating or chewing a bone 🐾 Playing with their toys 🐾 Unwell or injured 🐾 On their beds 🐾 In their crate, pen, or kennel	🐾 Play rough with a dog 🐾 Tease, pull hair, or hurt them 🐾 Handle them inappropriately or pick them up 🐾 Grab them around the neck 🐾 Squeeze or hug them 🐾 Wrestle them on the ground 🐾 Take food from their bowl or mouth

Some handy hints for children

🐾 **Holding a Puppy**

Before holding a puppy, a child should always sit down on the floor. Do not let a child under 10 pick up or carry a puppy. Remember, some puppies do not like to be held tightly and may wriggle and scratch.

🐾 **Patting a Puppy**

Children often want to hug a dog with their arms around its neck, but puppies do not like this. Teach your child to be gentle and stroke the dog from underneath their chin or along their back. Many dogs do not like being patted on the head. Teach your child that most dogs don't actually like hugs and kisses like we do and might enjoy a back scratch instead.

🐾 **Treats**

Older children can be taught how to make a puppy sit when giving a dog a treat. However, be aware that the dog may then jump or lunge to get the treat, which can be quite frightening. This activity should be supervised with an adult and practised.

🐾 **Supervising Play**

Children often run instead of walking; they love to be active. All these behaviours resemble the behaviour of other puppies, so a puppy may chase a child. Teach your child to walk and play quietly around your puppy until the puppy becomes more comfortable and calmer. Have your puppy on a lead when children are running around.

Standing still like a statue will usually stop a puppy jumping. You can teach children to "be a statue" by standing still, folding their arms, and looking away from the puppy. Your puppy will soon learn that "statues" aren't much fun to chase.

If the puppy is overexcited, apply common-sense management techniques such as putting the puppy away in a crate or pen with a tasty chew toy until things are a little more settled.

Make sure that the children spend just as much quiet time with the dog, such as patting and grooming, as they do play time. Most puppies love to be gently brushed and children really enjoy this activity.

Your child's toys

Your puppy does not know the difference between their toys and your child's toys. You and/or your child must take responsibility for keeping their playthings out of reach of your dog. Puppies love small toys like plastic Duplo, Lego, and little rubber balls, which can be lethal. Children's socks are also a favourite and easily swallowed, so please get children to pick these up. There may be quite a learning curve with this, so in the meantime, **use a baby gate or a pen to keep your puppy confined to one area of the house.**

SOCIALISATION OF YOUR PUPPY

Socialisation is the new buzzword! It means "learning to be part of society" and it is *so* important. If you teach your puppy nothing else, teach your puppy that the world is a safe and happy place. This means taking your puppy lots of places; exposing them to different sights, sounds, surfaces, humans and other animals; and making sure they are having a good time while doing so. Socialisation is *not* just about taking your puppy to meet other dogs.

You want to give your puppy a positive association with the world and all the things they are likely to encounter in their dog life. And you want to do it *now*. The primary socialisation window is alarmingly small – from 3–4 weeks to about 13–14 weeks. If you get your pup at 8 weeks, half that period is already gone – so hopefully the owner of the pup's mother has already laid a good socialisation foundation!

Most people understand the part about taking their puppy to lots of different places for socialisation. But they sometimes miss the critically important part:

Make sure your puppy has a good time.

Take your puppy to safe places where you can control the environment to a reasonable degree. Loud parties, dog parks, and crowded street markets are not a good idea. Small social gatherings, controlled groups of children, and well-run, force-free puppy classes are great. Find businesses that welcome pets (many hardware stores like Bunnings, Petbarn, and outdoor cafes are pet-friendly) and take them shopping or to school pick-up with you so they can meet lots of people. Until your puppy is fully vaccinated, always be careful in these kinds of situations and be sure to check that other dogs are fully vaccinated and healthy before allowing your puppy to say hi.

If your puppy seems fearful at any time, move them away from the fear-causing stimulus, let them observe from a safe distance, and feed high-value treats to help them build a good association with the thing, whatever it is. Then make a mental note (or keep a written list!) of things you want to help your puppy become more comfortable with by doing focused "counter-conditioning" sessions. (Use the puppy socialisation chart in the back of the book.)

Stages of Puppy Development

Birth to 7 weeks	A puppy needs sleep, food, and warmth. They need their mother for security and discipline, and their littermates for learning and socialisation. The puppy learns to function within a pack and learns order of dominance. They become aware of their environment. During this period puppies should be left with their mother.
8–12 weeks	A puppy is ready to leave their mother and siblings at 8 weeks. They now need socialising with the outside world. This is the age when a puppy goes through their first major "fear period", where they become extra sensitive to traumatic experiences. Introduce your puppy to as many different sights and sounds as possible, but always with a positive association, and remove them from any situations they find stressful. (And remember to keep puppy safe, as they are not fully vaccinated yet.)
12–16 weeks	Training and socialisation should begin now. **This is a critical period for socialising** with other humans, pets, places, and situations. Though the first fear period has theoretically already passed, fear can continue to set in at this age and frightening experiences can have a lasting effect. It is important to strive for nothing but positive interactions, to watch the puppy carefully, and to quickly remove the puppy from stressful or frightening situations. After 16 weeks the socialisation window closes, and it becomes much harder to get a puppy socialised.
4–8 months	A small "fear period" may occur at 4–8 months of age. It passes quickly, but a bad fright or experience during this time can traumatise a puppy. Continue training, socialising, and having lots of fun, but carefully avoid situations that may provoke fear.
8–14 months	This can be a stressful time for several reasons. This is when the second major fear period occurs, which can be more noticeable and longer. Again, do not push the puppy during this time. Your puppy may have her first season or get desexed. They are like teenagers and can be challenging in terms of their behaviour, perhaps testing the boundaries! Keep on with training and having fun and positive experiences.

At the back of the book is a **puppy socialisation chart** with a list of recommended experiences. You should try to expose your puppy to each experience at least four times a week. Use food reward, toys, and voice to praise. The goal is that the puppy has positive experiences, not neutral or bad ones. Watch your puppy's response and give treats and play to help ensure the exposure is a success.

Fear Periods

Fear periods are real and happen to all puppies. Some overcome these periods easily to the point that they are barely noticeable, others are affected more.

The first fear period: 8–12 weeks

During this first fear period, the puppy is overly sensitive to traumatic experiences, and a single scary event may be enough to traumatise them and have lifelong effects on their behaviour. The fear can be of anything – most commonly a person, animal, object, place, or sound. This fear period overlaps with when we are taking our puppy home, which is another reason why these first few weeks are so important. A puppy needs to have good experiences with everything. Do not overload them with scary things like a noisy vacuum cleaner or a stressful vet visit. Make everything fun.

How to make things better:

- Use food treats to make positive associations.
- Plug in an Adaptil DAP diffuser at home when you first bring your new puppy home. (This releases a synthetic version of a calming dog pheromone.)
- Make crate training fun with treats and toys.
- Make *everything* fun!
- Never force a puppy if they are scared.

Second fear period: 8–14 Months

While the 8–12-week puppy fear period is in some cases hardly noticed by puppy owners, the second fear period can have a much bigger impact, partly because your puppy is now a much bigger dog.

This fear period is thought to be tied to the dog's sexual maturity and growth spurts. This means that in large breeds like the Golden Retriever, it may occur later than in a smaller dog. This stage is also known as the "teenage period", mirroring how human teenagers often go off the rails for a period and become more challenging as their bodies and brains develop. Reactivity levels rise during this stage, and owners often report that fear seems to pop out of nowhere. Dogs appear fearful of things they have seen or experienced before, including objects like rubbish bins, cars, or even people that previously did not trigger any significant reactions.

As in the first fear period, it is best to avoid traumatic experiences during this time, such as visits to the vet, moving to a new house, renovations, and any other potentially overwhelming experiences.

Tips for dealing with fear periods

- Do not overwhelm your puppy; take it slowly
- Avoid traumatic experiences
- Socialise, socialise, socialise
- Build confidence with training, playing, and having plenty of fun.

When fear strikes…

- Remain as calm as possible, as if it is no big deal
- "Counter-condition" by giving treats or playing
- Let the dog work it out on their own; be patient

❤ Do not punish the fear.

If you are uncertain or concerned, seek professional help from a dog trainer.

Puppies and Other Pets

Golden Retrievers usually get on very well with other pets and, if introduced at a young age, they can become best friends. We have had guinea pigs, cats, and chickens that have all co-existed well. Occasionally you will get a dog with a strong hunting instinct, and you will need to be more careful if they are introduced at an older age. (Being gundogs, some Golden Retrievers can be tempted by chickens!)

Ollie & Frith – best friends

Introducing puppies to other pets

If possible, start on a neutral territory, or outside. If you have cats, always make sure the cats have a place to get away, somewhere in the house that the puppy cannot get to. Discourage chasing until they are comfortable with each other.

Cats and dogs usually become best mates and will often groom each other and sleep together. You can buy baby gates with little cat doors; these work well for segregating cats from dogs.

If you have an older dog, introduce a puppy outside. Supervise all interaction for a few days. Expect that an older dog may feel rather put out by having a new family member. They may even tell a puppy off, especially if the

puppy takes the older dog's favourite toy or bone. While they settle in, do not leave out any food or toys that may cause a disagreement.

Feed the dogs apart and always supervise so your puppy does not attempt to eat the older dog's food. This is yet another situation where crate training is particularly useful, as the puppy can safely be put into their crate to give the older dog some peace and quiet.

When you bring a puppy into a household with an older dog, it is especially important to monitor play. All play should be supervised until 9–12 months. A large, boisterous adult can injure a puppy's soft, delicate bones very easily. **Do not allow rough play.**

I highly recommend that your puppy has their own area for when you are not home, especially if being left outside with an adult dog. If your adult dog is elderly and has health problems, remember they may also need space and rest. Introducing a playful, demanding puppy to their lives may not be what they want. In some cases a senior dog may not cope with a puppy at all, and it's also possible they may require more of your time, so you need to carefully consider what is best for them – and that may mean waiting to get a new puppy.

TRAINING AND BEHAVIOUR PROBLEMS

Puppy Play and Fun

Only ever use positive training methods. Training should always be fun. As soon as it is not fun for you, it is not fun for your puppy either. Modern training methods have changed, and we now know reward-based training is by far the most effective. Sure enough, Golden Retrievers respond very well to this method. How would you want to be trained if you were a puppy or child? You would want to feel safe, valued, and loved.

Now that positive training has come into its own, food is the most common type of reward. I always have food rewards in my pockets, so I can offer treats to reinforce my dogs whenever the opportunity presents itself. We all want to make good stuff happen! So you can expect your pup to focus their efforts on figuring out what they need to do to get you to give them treats. That is a good thing! It means that if you are good at reinforcing the behaviours you want, and not reinforcing the behaviours you don't want, you should ultimately get the results you are looking for (most of the time!).

After puppy preschool and puppy socialisation, it is essential to continue with training, either with the same organisation or with another training or obedience club. Continued training could be the most important thing you teach and affirm to your dog throughout their life. The tricky part is finding a training school you are happy with! Do seek recommendations, and use only qualified, force-free trainers. There are suggested links and training books in Appendix 3. This is not a training book; I have left that to the experts.

You should be committed to force-free, fear-free, and pain-free handling and training. Do not ever let anyone talk you into treating your puppy badly. No leash jerks, no shock collars, no "alpha rolls". Ever. Stick to your guns; there is always another way.

If your animal care and/or training professional insists that the use of pain or force is necessary, find another one. Plenty of professionals out there will support and respect your wishes when it comes to handling your dog. Your puppy cannot speak for themselves, and they are counting on you to do right by them.

Training rewards

If you can use part of your puppy's daily kibble allowance for training, that's ideal, but some puppies need something of higher reward. Some of the best food training treats you can use are air-dried meat such as **Ziwi Peak** (this comes in small pieces made in NZ) and a bag will last a long time. The fish or tripe varieties are well loved by dogs but do smell. Popular soft treats include **Prime dog rolls, tasty cheese, Devon sausage** or **small cocktail Frankfurts**. You can cut these up into small pieces and freeze in small bags for use when required.

Just remember that if you are handing out treats, they count as part of your puppy's total food intake for the day. Many people will see food as the only type of training reward, but remember, the puppy views many more things as "rewards" than just treats. Toys and play, praise, access in- and outside, mealtimes, enrichment, attention from visitors, coming out of a crate, getting out of the car, social experiences. We call these "life rewards" and it's important to include them as part of your rewards system.

Using a clicker

Clicker training is a common form of positive reinforcement for dogs. This simple and effective training method utilises a small device that trainers press to click when the dog shows a desired behaviour. The click is much faster and more distinct than saying "good dog" and much more effective than training with treats alone.

By pressing the clicker when your dog exhibits good behavior, and following up with a treat, your pup learns to associate the noise with a reward. A clicker helps your dog identify the very instant that they're doing what you want them to do, making their learning process faster.

Once the dog learns the positive effects of the clicking sound, the clicker itself acts as a conditioned reinforcer. Clickers can be found at most major pet stores and are relatively inexpensive.

Using a tug toy

Playing tug with your puppy has many benefits, including helping you bond with your puppy, facilitating training, providing mental stimulation, and burning off some of that boundless energy. And contrary to popular belief, it will not create aggression. On the contrary, it can improve impulse control. I use a tug during training as a reward and to keep my puppy motivated.

More and more trainers are using tug toys, and most dogs love them, but there are some guidelines to follow in order to get the most benefit from them:

🐾 Be gentle – never pull harder than the dog. With puppies you need to be extra careful, as their teeth and jaw are developing, and you could cause serious harm if you do not play responsibly.
🐾 You initiate the game, not the dog.
🐾 Your training toys are special and reserved for training time only.
🐾 Teach your dog to drop it or give when you want to stop.
🐾 Use a tug during training as a reward and to keep your puppy motivated.

First Commands

"Sit"

"Sit" is the first and most important command you should teach your puppy. "Sit" is used in so many different facets of a puppy's life. It's the one (fairly) simple way to resolve or prevent a whole host of annoying behaviours – jumping up, barking, scratching at the back door. Just teach your dog to sit!

It's useful to teach your dog that they are always expected to sit in particular situations, including:

🐾 Sit before play
🐾 Sit before greeting people
🐾 Sit to go in and out of doors
🐾 Sit to cross roads
🐾 Sit before cuddles and attention
🐾 Sit before dinner
🐾 Sit for children's attention
🐾 Sit to clip the lead on and off.

"Sit" can easily be taught using a food reward. If you hold a treat above a puppy's nose and raise your hand slightly over their head, they will usually automatically sit. Then praise and reward. Easy!

"Come" (Recall)

Recall (coming when called) may just be the single most important behaviour you can teach your puppy. A dog who has a solid recall can be given more freedom to run and play in areas where dogs are allowed off leash. Dogs who get to run and play are generally much healthier, both physically and mentally, and much easier to live with, as they can burn off excess energy by running around. A tired dog means a happy owner! And you never know, a solid recall might just save your dog's life someday.

Make sure your recall cue always means "good stuff", such as a chance to play with a highly valued toy or high-value treats. Never call your dog to you to do something they don't love, like giving a pill, treating ears, or putting them in their crate. Certainly, never call them to you to punish or even just scold them.

Unlike old-fashioned training, where you face your dog, command them to come, and jerk on the leash if they do not come, today's positive trainer teaches recall as another fun game to play with humans. Play "Run Away Come" by calling the dog and then walking or running away fast, so the puppy comes galloping and romping after their human and gets to party with treats and/or toys when they catch up. The puppy learns that "Come!" is an irresistible invitation to play the chase game, which always ends in a reward. In the early days it can be helpful to use a "long line" for recall training, which ensures the puppy has freedom, but still gives you control.

Lead walking

You're probably very excited to take your new puppy out for a walk as soon as possible. But should you use a collar, harness, or head collar?

Personally, **I prefer to start a puppy on a soft flat collar** and lead with a small clip. This gives you very good control. Flat collars are usually made of nylon or leather with a buckle. Other types of collars include slip and Martingale collars, but these can put more pressure on the neck and are not as suitable for puppies.

A soft harness is also suitable for a young puppy to start training on. It doesn't provide quite as good control as a collar, but initially training is mostly about getting them to focus on you, so this isn't a big problem. The main benefit of a harness is that it does not put any pressure on the throat. Harnesses work well for some dogs, but not so well for others, who will pull even more. A front-clip harness gives you much more control than a back-clip harness, which can make dogs pull. It is also important to choose a harness that does not restrict shoulder and elbow movement, and fits comfortably.

Head collars are not suitable for young puppies. Head collars or "halters" work by wrapping around the nose, giving the handler greater control over the head by putting pressure on the nose. I do not recommend a head collar until at least 6 months of age. You must gradually condition a puppy to get used to a head collar, otherwise they will fight it and try and get it off. Conditioning involves putting the head collar on for short periods indoors and letting the puppy walk around with it, using food rewards to distract them from the collar. Once they are comfortable you can attach the lead and encourage them to walk with you. This process may take a few days.

Common Behaviour Problems

Puppy biting (mouthing)

"Help, my puppy is biting me! What can I do?"

Every breeder has heard this a million times over! It's the most common question in my puppy group. Play biting or mouthing hurts, but remember, it is not forever. It is part of a puppy's development and something all puppies do. Their mouth is equivalent to a toddler's hands. Yes, I know it can hurt! But I repeat: *It is normal puppy development.*

Unfortunately, as they no longer have their brothers and sisters to chew and bite, you have become their playmate... and their target! Distraction is the key. As soon as your puppy starts to chew your hands or feet, distract with a soft toy in your other hand. Keep the toy interesting; move it around. A tug toy can be fun, as long as you play gently and do not let them get overexcited.

If your puppy loves to play bite, avoid handling them when they are overaroused. Often an overtired puppy in the evening will become overexcited and biting can be quite full-on. When a puppy is like this, they need time out in a quiet place or their crate (with a chew toy). **Inappropriate behaviour means time out.**

Avoid situations where the puppy will "win". For example, do not pick a puppy up when they do not want to be picked up. They may bite, so you drop them or put them down, so they think, "Great, that worked!" Instead, wait until they are relaxed and then pick them up. Also remember that some puppies just do not like to be cuddled.

When a puppy is relaxed, try stroking them gently. Offer them some treats and have a toy ready so that if they get mouthy you can offer it to them. If they bite, give a loud "ouch" then walk away. Leave the room for a few minutes. A puppy will soon learn that you bring the good stuff. Never use pain or an "alpha roll" (where you force your dog into a submissive position) to discourage mouthing. Remember, it is a normal part of being a puppy.

Humping

Puppies may mount and hump their littermates, other playmates, people, and toys. Humping is often caused by energy arousal and overexcitement. It is not a sexual thing in a young puppy, and girls do it just as often as boys. Distract your puppy, and if they are trying to hump your leg or child then remove them from the situation. They may need time out, or redirection with a game of tug or a Kong toy.

Jumping up

Jumping up is a normal behaviour for puppies. Watch them with their mother – they jump up to her for attention, so it is a natural progression to want to jump up at us for attention… and often they get it. Initially we think it is cute, but as they get larger it becomes less so. Certainly, a 35 kg dog jumping on a child or a dog with muddy feet jumping on you just as you are leaving for work would hardly be described as cute!

The best and quickest way to train your puppy not to jump up is to ignore them when they do. Turn away, avoid eye contact, and when they do sit, praise and offer a treat. I use clicker training for this. It is amazing just how quickly a puppy learns that if they sit, they get a click and treat. If they jump up, they don't. The more consistent you can be with this, the more effective it will be, so the whole family (and visitors!) need to be in on this.

If you struggle with an overexcited puppy when you have visitors, keep him on a lead when they arrive. Ask the visitor to stand still to say hello, then get the puppy's attention and say, "Sit." Then, of course, give the puppy a treat when they sit.

Sitting is the command that overcomes jumping, and any number of other behaviours. A puppy can quickly learn to sit whenever they meet someone, before coming in the door, or in any other situation.

Resource guarding

Resource guarding is display of aggressive behaviour designed to scare people off. It is usually over a toy or a valued item such as food. What may happen is you place the puppy's food bowl down, and if you go to reach out they growl, as they feel the need to guard it. In canine law this would be normal behaviour. People think because you have a sweet little Golden Retriever puppy that this should not happen, but occasionally it does and unfortunately it seems to be a problem on the increase. The concerning part is that we are now hearing of puppies being surrendered because of this behaviour. But if you deal with it quickly and correctly, it can be solved very quickly.

As soon as you get your puppy, start working on exchanging toys and even food. Never snatch objects like socks or children's toys from a pup's mouth. Instead, calmly say, "Give" or "Thank you", put a treat under their nose, and gently take the object. If you do observe resource guarding, it is critical to act quickly. If your puppy shows any sign of aggression when you approach their bowl, do not attempt to take it, as this may escalate the situation. A puppy needs to be taught that a human or baby crawling towards their food bowl is not a threat.

The key with resource guarding is to offer **higher-value treats** in exchange for what they have in their mouth. Feed them half their dinner and reserve the yummiest bits. Place their bowl on the ground and allow them to eat, then move away and return once they have finished. If they show discomfort or growl, toss some of the saved food into their bowl and repeat the sequence. Soon they will be looking for you to approach their food bowl, as they know you will bring more yummy food. This training should be done when the puppy is in a relaxed mood. If they are overexcited, they will be less responsive to training.

The aim is to get them to feel comfortable with you being around when they are eating and not to see you as a threat. It can also help to hand feed a puppy sometimes rather than just feeding them in a bowl, or put their food in a treat dispensing ball so they must work for it.

Do not let children attempt this. A dog should be fed in a quiet place away from children and other pets. Do not use any type of physical punishment, as this will make the whole situation much worse.

If you feel you cannot cope with this problem, please seek early help from a professional dog trainer.

Barking

Barking is often associated with boredom and anxiety. It is a problem that we are often asked about and can also be a public nuisance (not surprisingly, it is the most common complaint neighbours make about dogs), so it must be taken seriously.

In the next chapter I talk about canine enrichment and offer options to alleviate boredom. These are your first options, and for many dogs giving them something to do is enough to alleviate boredom and prevent excessive barking.

A possum on the fence or cat walking by will usually get a response, and this is natural. (We used to have a possum that came out every night and taunted my dogs, they would go crazy. It became a bit of a problem!)

Here are some **tips for dealing with inappropriate barking:**

- 🐾 Stay calm – if you answer your dog by raising your voice or yelling, they will think you are trying to join in. Instead, say in a quiet but firm voice, "Thank you, I heard you, and quiet!"
- 🐾 Use a command word like "Quiet" or "Stop". Reward when the dog stops.
- 🐾 Ignore it – not easy, but with a puppy, try! The second barking stops, reward with lots of praise.
- 🐾 Distract them. Give them a command for something they *can* do, like sit or drop, and reward.
- 🐾 Mask the stimulus – block out sounds using a radio or TV and block out sights using curtains or furniture, or better still, solid fences so they cannot see activity on the street or from the neighbours.
- 🐾 Tire them out – mentally and physically. Offer enrichment toys (see *Enrichment Games (Entertainment)*, page 47) and daily exercise. Enrichment toys like a stuffed Kong can keep a dog occupied for several hours.

If barking becomes a real problem, it may be worth seeking professional advice from a qualified dog trainer.

Pulling on the lead

Pulling on the lead is not usually a baby puppy problem, but often at about 5–6 months of age your adolescent puppy will suddenly become more confident and decide they want to march along ahead of you and pull you around, to sniff or to meet people or other dogs. This is when we are often asked about collars and harnesses to stop the pulling.

If you attend puppy school and further training, hopefully you will master lead walking early and be ready to get straight on top of any issues with pulling. However, if you find it is a real problem, you could try a front-clip harness or a Gentle Leader head collar or similar (only after gradually conditioning them to it and never before 6 months of age). There are many different brands of front-clip harnesses on the market, so ask your trainer for advice. Look for a harness that does not restrict the shoulders or rub under the elbows avoid back clip harnesses as they simply do not give you good control, and encourage pulling.

Poop eating

Owners are often horrified to see their beautiful puppy (or adult dog!) eating their own poop. Surprisingly, it is quite common and is not necessarily due to any dietary deficiencies. This is an innate behaviour in dogs, so it can be a hard habit to break. It tends to be more common in multiple dog households.

The best advice I can offer is to buy a pooper scooper and be ready to scoop up your dog's poo as soon as you see them pooping. Many people have tried adding pineapple, enzymes, or other additives to a dog's diet, and the consensus is nothing reliably works. Most dogs just seem to grow out of it... though some don't!

Separation Anxiety

Separation anxiety refers to the distress some dogs feel when they are separated from you, and is far and away the most common form of anxiety in dogs. Dogs associate everything they value (such as company, food, play, walks) with people, so they learn and expect that when they are left alone they won't get any of that good stuff. Unless they have been taught how to cope with being away from their humans, they can suffer anxiety.

Common signs of separation anxiety

Dogs with separation anxiety will often show some of the following signs when the owner is not home:

- Barking or howling
- Panting or pacing
- Digging
- Escaping the yard (or trying to)
- Destroying furniture or other things
- Self-harm, including licking or chewing
- Not eating
- Shivering, lip licking, yawning.

Dogs are social animals. In a world not controlled by humans, our dogs would spend most of their time in the company of their canine friends. In contrast, in our world, a significant proportion of dogs are "only children" and are left home alone for 8– 10 hours at a time, sometimes even longer. The incidence of separation anxiety in our doggy companions is a sad testimony to this, and a serious problem.

The best time for teaching a dog to learn to cope with being alone is when they are a puppy. To avoid separation anxiety, gradually introduce your puppy to short periods of being alone. Include crate or exercise-pen training as part of this process, so they can be left safely confined while you are away. Plan to take at least a week off work after your pup arrives so you can help get them accustomed to longer and longer periods alone.

Before you leave your puppy alone, play with them to tire them out, then put them in their crate or pen and give them a high-value chew such as a food-stuffed Kong or other yummy, long-lasting treat. Sit nearby, reading or working on your computer for a few minutes, then slowly move away from the puppy until you are out of sight. After 30 seconds, come back into the room (if they are settled or sleeping, do not disturb). Continue to do this on a regular basis, gradually increasing the speed at which you move away and the length of time you leave them alone, until they are able to remain calm and relaxed on their own. The next step is to actually leave the house. Pop out for 15–30 minutes the first time, and build up to an hour or more. It's a good idea to set up a camera so you can see how your puppy is coping. If your puppy is going through a fear period, it's important to slow down if you notice them becoming distressed at all.

Purchase an Adaptil diffuser for the room where your puppy spends most of their time. This is like a fragrance diffuser, but instead it releases a calming canine pheromone, which has a calming effect on dogs but is undetectable to us. Adaptil is also available as a collar, though anecdotally this doesn't seem to be as effective as a diffuser.

Whenever you are not with them, make sure your puppy has plenty to keep them busy. The section below on enrichment will give you some ideas.

If your dog develops separation anxiety despite the above training, you should seek help from an animal trainer or behaviourist earlier rather than later – the longer the anxiety and associated behaviours go on, the more ingrained they become.

Car Travel

Dogs who have difficulty with car travel usually fall into one of two categories: those who have motion sickness and those with a fear of riding in the car. Thankfully most Golden Retrievers love car rides, but as puppies it is quite common for them to suffer from car sickness. So what is the best way to get your puppy accustomed to car rides and prevent these issues?

Puppies, like children, are more prone to motion sickness than adults. This is because their inner ear is not yet fully developed. Most dogs eventually grow out of this problem, but if your puppy starts to drool or vomit when you hit the road, there are a few steps you can take to remedy the situation.

- 🐾 Spend some time getting your puppy used to being in a crate in the car.
- 🐾 Once they are relaxed with this, take them for short trips around the block, with lots of praise at the end. Gradually increase the travel distance.
- 🐾 Avoid sudden stops and winding roads until they are comfortable.
- 🐾 Limit your puppy's food and water intake for a couple of hours before the trip.
- 🐾 Whenever you put your puppy in the car, offer some treats or a Kong toy to distract them and create a good association.
- 🐾 Roll down the car windows so fresh air can flow into the car.
- 🐾 If they regularly feel unwell in the car, they will start to become anxious about going in the car, so you should try something to reduce nausea. Natural remedies you can try include Rescue Remedy drops (I've found these work well), Adaptil spray in the crate, and ginger tablets. However, if these don't work, you can ask your vet about medication for motion sickness.

Safety: Dogs must wear a car harness or be in the back of a wagon/SUV with a barrier.

Bored dogs get into trouble. We are their main souce of entertainment, so if we do not give them fun things to do they will will come up with their own activities… which may include chewing shoes, digging holes, chewing plants or furniture, or excessive barking! We need to find ways to keep our puppy (or adult dog) happy, healthy, and busy, especially when we are not around. Simply adding a few mentally stimulating enrichment games to your dog's daily routine can make a world of difference to their wellbeing and behaviour.

Some of my favourite boredom busters: snuffle mat, Kong, Kong wobbler, tug toys, chew bone, lick mat

We all know a tired dog is a good dog, but this does not have to mean doing an hour-long run! A dog can be made mentally tired by playing brain games, which again, doesn't have to mean razzing them up. Low-arousal activities like sniffing and licking are ways of exercising the brain that can be quite calming. Just like human children, dogs need a balance of physical and mental exercise.

Enrichment Toys and Games

Below are some suggestions to keep your puppy or dog busy and entertained – and distracted from the things they shouldn't be doing – throughout the day. **When trying the suggestions that involve food, always remember that any food used forms part of your puppy's daily calorie allowance.**

Stuffed Kong and West Paw Toppl

Kongs come in many shapes and forms, including soft toys, but here I am referring to the original rubber Kong (the blue toy in the photo above). A stuffed Kong is the easiest way to keep a dog mentally stimulated and busy with minimal effort – they're even dishwasher safe! I use a Kong whenever I want my dogs to be relaxed inside.

There are many different stuffing options, but one of my favourites is a chunk of tasty cheese and peanut butter. This lasts a long time. Another good option is to fill the Kong with banana, yoghurt, and peanut butter then freeze it. Freezing is a great idea if your dog becomes an expert at unstuffing a Kong!

You can also use canned dog food, cream cheese, Prime dog roll, kibble, pumpkin, apple, carrot, banana, or Kong stuffing. Always remember these are all contributing calories to your dog's daily total, so account for this when you measure out your dog's meals. Always wash Kongs after every use.

West Paw Toppl

West Paw Toppls are very similar to Kongs. They come in many shapes and sizes and can be filled with food and frozen. Some dogs enjoy these more as they require less work to get the food reward. You can even feed your puppy their meals via a Toppl. Soak their kibble and add fruits, yoghurt, or a chew. You can get quite creative with what you use to fill it!

Food-dispensing toys

Another fun activity for dogs is to get their food from a food-dispensing toy. Some of my favourites are the Starmark Bob-A-Lot, Kong Wobbler, and Kong Gyro (shown below).

I often feed my puppies their kibble from the Wobbler, and let them tire themselves out chasing it around to get all their food! This toy is also excellent for dogs who wolf down their food. The Bob-A-Lot can hold 2 cups of kibble and takes hours to empty. It may seem strange making a dog work for their food, but in the wild this is natural, and they also love this game.

Kong toys and a snuffle mat

Hide and seek

Dogs love to play hide and seek. Hide toys or treats around the house or outside. They will have so much fun giving their nose a workout to find the treats – and they'll get nice and tired in the process! Hiding toys is also a fun way to get the kids involved.

Kibble trail or scatter feeding

Instead of feeding your dog their dry food in a bowl, go outside and make a trail around the backyard. They will have a great time following the trail and finding their food. Scatter feeding is a great low-arousal activity that has a calming effect. It is good mental exercise, and is particularly useful if you are leaving a dog or puppy alone for a while outside, as it will take their mind off you being gone.

Frozen dog treats

When it comes to canine enrichment, nothing is easier than frozen dog treats. Dogs love these, especially on a warm day. They are well suited to use outdoors in summer. You can freeze treats made up of yoghurt, banana, pumpkin, peanut butter, or even fruit. You can freeze the treats in different size cups or even bowls or pans depending on how long you need to keep them occupied!

Snuffle mats

A few years ago no one knew what a snuffle mat was, but these days they are very popular. I don't know who invented them, but I take my hat off to them! They are so simple – just a rubber mat (often a doormat) with lots of fabric (usually fleece) strips tied to it. Many crafty people make their own, but you can find them for sale on Facebook and eBay. As you can see in this photo, you can be quite creative!

The concept is that you can sprinkle kibble or any dry treat throughout the mat, and the dog "snuffles" it out. It is a fun way for a dog to get its food. Use under supervision, as some dogs quite enjoy eating the rubber mat once all the treats were gone – I speak from experience! A more basic substitute for a snuffle mat is a rolled towel – just roll the treats up in it and let them at it! (If you do this you'll want to make sure you keep your own towels well out of reach!)

Digging pit

Dogs love to dig, so give them somewhere to dig or they might just choose your veggie patch or flower bed! Designated an area just for them, or even fill a child's plastic sandpit and encourage your puppy to dig by burying toys or treats. Praise them when they dig, and let them have fun. You will be surprised how quickly they adapt to this.

Puzzle toys

These are an easy way to keep your dog entertained and are fun for a child to interact with as well. However, they should only be used under supervision, as many of them can be chewed up and swallowed. There are so many different puzzle toys available, but there are also many toys you can make yourself – just Google it! Children can have lots of fun making these from cardboard tubes, egg cartons, boxes, or plastic bottles.

Enrichment Activities

Doggie daycare

A professional, well-run doggie daycare offers many advantages for dogs whose owners work and do not want their dogs to be alone all day. Daycare alleviates boredom and loneliness, and offers a safe, interactive, fun, cage-free outlet for high-energy dogs. Not all dogs are suited to daycare – if you have an anxious or aggressive dog then daycare is not for them.

It is important you visit a few daycare centres and see how they are run. Ideally dogs should be split into small groups based on age and size. There should be constant supervision. I have seen some excellent daycare centres and some very poor ones, so do your homework and ask for recommendations from friends.

Puppy parties

Puppy parties can be a lot of fun and are extremely popular. They are a great way to get a group of puppies together for socialisation. Always supervise and only let a couple of well-matched puppies play at a time, as one big bully of a puppy can terrify a smaller or timid puppy and cause ongoing problems. Puppies must be removed for time out at the first hint of aggression.

Dog parks

Dog parks are very popular and can be great fun and a good way to socialise your dog, but they also have high risks. Unfortunately, irresponsible people often bring along dogs with no social skills, which can be aggressive and out of control. In a dog park, your dog cannot escape if it is being hassled by other dogs. Always watch your dog very carefully, and watch the dogs in the park for a few minutes to identify any potential problems before you let your own dog in.

I do not recommend taking a puppy to a dog park, as one bad experience could really traumatise them. Many adult dogs simply do not like puppies, and it is easy for a puppy to get trapped in a corner. If you have a dog that suffers from anxiety, avoid dog parks altogether. Like people who don't like large groups, they could find the whole situation incredibly stressful.

There are some excellent privately owned dog parks, with swimming pools and fun agility structures for dogs to play on. These are a safer way to go, as you can arrange a private gathering of like-minded people and dogs. Check out the social meet-up dog groups on Facebook.

Teaching your puppy to swim

Golden Retrievers usually love to swim; after all, they were bred to retrieve game from water. Swimming is non-impact exercise, so it is easy on the joints. This makes it an excellent form of exercise for puppies and for older dogs with joint problems.

When introducing a puppy to water, start by letting them explore puddles and flat water on their own. Often their natural curiosity will get the better of them and they will be like a duck to water!

Another way to get them enjoying water is to take them out with an older dog that loves water and see if they will follow. Choose a place with shallow water to begin with and always watch carefully, as some do not instantly swim. I highly recommend a dog life jacket for teaching a puppy to swim. There are many dog pools that teach puppies to swim, which is a great idea and is becoming extremely popular.

You can buy absorbent **dog drying coats**, which are excellent for putting on a dog after they have been swimming. If you take your puppy to the beach, remember to rinse the salt and sand from their coat and dry them well so they do not get irritated skin or develop a skin infection (known as a "hot spot").

Dog Sports

Dog sports are a great way to enjoy the outdoors and bond with your dog. Dog sports worldwide include:

- 🐾 Agility
- 🐾 Competition Obedience
- 🐾 Conformation Showing
- 🐾 Dances with Dogs
- 🐾 EarthDog
- 🐾 Field Trails
- 🐾 FlyBall

- 🐾 Herding
- 🐾 I Endurance
- 🐾 Lure Coursing
- 🐾 Nose work
- 🐾 Rally
- 🐾 Retrieving
- 🐾 Scentwork

- 🐾 Sled Sports
- 🐾 Tracking
- 🐾 Trick Dogs
- 🐾 Tribal
- 🐾 Track and Search

As you can see, there is something for every dog and handler, from formal conformation showing through to the "thinking" dog sports of obedience, tracking, trialling, Dances with Dogs, Rally, agility, and jumping (and the list goes on!). These are all kennel club–sanctioned events. I could fill a book writing about all the activities available to you. If you are interested in any of these events it is a good idea to join a local obedience club, which should be able to offer advice and training. Even if your Golden Retriever does not have pedigree papers, you can still compete in many of these competitions as an associate member.

If you'd like to find out more about dog competitions, please see Appendix 3 for a list of kennel clubs.

There are also some more casual, fun events you can do, such as dock jumping, which Goldens simply love. Dock jumping, also known as dock diving, is a dog sport in which dogs compete to jump the longest distance or greatest height from a dock into a body of water. Dock jumping events are gaining traction in Australia, and are becoming a popular spectator sport.

Therapy Dogs and Assistance Dogs

Many people purchase a Golden Retriever puppy with the intention of training them to becoming a therapy or even an assistance dog. What this means varies between countries, but here we will look at what therapy, assistance, and emotional support dogs do in Australia.

- 🐾 **Therapy Dogs** work with a handler to provide comfort and joy to people in hospital, schools, aged-care facilities, courts, and so on. Therapy dogs are usually specialised in a certain area, for example, "Storybook dogs" or school therapy dogs. They usually offer support to many different people in the community, rather than a specific person. Therapy dogs do not have guaranteed access to all public places or transport.

- 🐾 **Service Dogs (Assistance Dogs)** are trained to provide individualised, specialised support for handlers with specific physical or mental disabilities (e.g. impaired hearing or eyesight, autism, PTSD) or medical conditions (e.g. epilepsy, cardiovascular disease). Dogs undergo intensive training, usually over 2 years, to perform particular tasks to assist their handlers. Once they are working at the required level, assistance dogs are certified and gain public access rights to accompany their owner anywhere under the *Disability Discrimination Act 1992*. The owner must carry a registration card.

- 🐾 **Emotional Support Animals (ESAs) or Companion Dogs** give comfort and support to handlers with anxiety, disability, or emotional-related illness. They are not specifically trained to provide support; rather, they do so merely by their presence. Unlike assistance dogs, ESAs are not certified, are not recognised under Australian law, and are not guaranteed public access. The term is vague, with no definition or behaviour standards.

If you are looking for a dog to train as a Therapy or Assistance Dog, you will need to find a qualified trainer to prepare you and your dog for the Public Access Test. They will also provide honest feedback on the suitability of your dog as a service or therapy dog – and there's no guarantee they will be suitable. Anxious or fearful dogs are not suitable for testing. As mentioned in the section on choosing a puppy, you should be upfront with the breeder about your needs so they can arrange for you to receive a puppy that is suitable as a Therapy or Assistance Dog.

THE TEENAGE YEARS

From 8 months to about 3 years, I compare Golden Retrievers to teenagers: full-of-life, mischievous risk takers that can be quite challenging at times!

Many people think once they get through the initial puppy phase their puppy will suddenly transform into a well-trained, socially acceptable young adult. Often this does not happen! This phase can be quite challenging, as your adolescent dog is much larger and harder to control than when they were a puppy. Hormones are racing and the brain is growing and developing, just like it does in human teenagers.

It is especially important to keep up with training during this time, and to give your "teenage" dog guidelines on how to behave. Bonding time is very important, too. You may need to go back to basics to enforce behaviours.

Dog trainers are often contacted as people find their well-behaved puppy has suddenly turned into an unruly teenager.

Exercise and mind games are more important than ever. Chewing is relaxing to a dog, so although teething is over, make sure they have safe chew toys (see the *Enrichment Games (Entertainment)*, page 47, for ideas). Make sure that if you are at work, you leave activities for your dog to do – otherwise you may find they have made their own fun!

Remember, a tired dog is a happy dog – but this does not need to be from exercise. Mental stimulation is hard work for a dog as well. Your dog is still growing, and you'll need to continue to protect their joints until they are 12–18 months of age, so be mindful of how much physical exercise they are getting. Make sure your dog still gets plenty of sleep: Adolescent dogs seem to have boundless energy, but they still need sleep like the rest of us!

Sammi & Millie

Socialisation is still very important – don't stop now just because they are a teenager. Avoid dog parks and places where you do not know the other dogs, as this can make your dog more reactive. Remember that adolescence often coincides with a fear period, and be aware that they may become scared of things that never bothered them before, including certain people and/or objects such as cars.

Hormones are racing, and most vets will recommend you have your dog desexed. This may go some way to helping with behaviour, and certainly eliminating sexual hormones takes one thing off their mind, especially in male dogs. But testosterone is not the be-all and end-all of hormones, and even desexed dogs will still go through behaviour problems at this stage of life. As mentioned earlier, we do recommend that you leave desexing until your dog has reached full maturity if possible.

Nothing is more beautiful than a Golden Retriever with a gleaming, luxurious coat of cream and gold. But there is a price to pay for everything, and with a Golden it is grooming. Golden Retrievers have a double coat: a soft, dense undercoat, and a coarser, water-repellent outer coat that may be wavy. All Goldens have the trademark "feathering" (tufts of hair with a feathery appearance), which starts to develop at around 3 months of age.

You may have heard the expression "I don't shed, I emit magical fibres of joy and love!" Goldens are high maintenance when it comes to keeping them clean and tidy. They are *not* the right breed for someone who is super house-proud and does not like dog hair. Yes, they do shed a lot of hair, and your house (and clothes) will always have those magical fibres on the floor... so invest in a good vacuum cleaner! Goldens also love running outdoors, and seem to be drawn to mud and water like a magnet!

Grooming does not mean just a quick tickle with the brush once a week. It is a special time and is important for bonding as well as checking for any lumps or bumps, skin infections, grass seeds, ear problems, overgrown nails, or dental disease.

Start grooming your puppy with a soft brush from 8 weeks, so they learn to enjoy it. Play with their feet and toes, check their teeth and ears, and run your hands over every part of their body. Use treats to reward them and make it fun. This will make grooming them as an adult much easier for both of you.

Archie during his spring de-shedding groom

Bathing

Dogs should not be bathed too often, as it strips the natural oils from the coat, but your Golden will require a bath from time to time when they get smelly or dirty. As a guideline, you should bathe your dog no more often than once a fortnight, and bathing every 1–2 months is more appropriate. Your dog will also require some trimming occasionally to stop his coat matting and to keep his feet tidy. This reduces muddy feet and reduces the chance of skin infections between the toes. You can do this yourself or visit a groomer 2–3 times a year.

Wash them in warm water and use a dog shampoo. Human shampoos are not pH balanced for dogs and can dry the skin out or cause reactions. If your puppy is itchy or has sensitive skin, use a natural or oatmeal-based shampoo such as Aloveen or Epi-Soothe.

Wet your puppy all over then massage the shampoo throughout the coat and rinse well. If your puppy is very dirty you may need to rinse and repeat. Once the coat is clean, apply a dog conditioner to condition the coat and stop it from drying out.

Use a towel, drying coat (such as the excellent Surf Dog drying coats, which mop up a lot of excess water), dog dryer, or heater to dry your dog. If it is a nice sunny day you can let them dry naturally, but watch they don't roll in the dirt!

When you have a new puppy, it is a good idea to bath them monthly, so they get used to it. You can either do this at home, take them to a pet store, or visit a groomer. Either way, you want it to be a nice, positive experience for your puppy, so take lots of treats and try to avoid stress. Often it is the dryer they find most frightening, so drying with a towel, in front of the heater, or in the sun may be easier initially. A dryer should be introduced gradually. Your early training will make a groomer's job much easier.

Hint: A good way to avoid shampoo wastage is to dilute shampoo with water (1 part shampoo to 4 parts water) in an old sauce bottle. This makes the shampoo go much further.

The Grooming Procedure

A pet groom usually involves a bath, then a basic tidy-up trim of the feet, nails, legs, and tail; thinning out of the hair around the ears and neck; and brushing out of all loose hair and knots. The following page shows you how to do this yourself. It is not difficult if you have the right tools.

Note that this is what's known as a "pet trim", and it is quite different from a "show trim", which is much more involved. A show trim is used to present the Golden Retriever at its best and emphasise its body structure when it is presented to the judge. If you visit a dog show you will see that the dogs are trimmed carefully around the neck, ears, legs and feet, and their coats are perfectly smooth and very tidy, with not a hair out of place! Show grooming is a professional job and takes many hours.

Step 1: Bathing

If your puppy or dog is dirty, I recommend bathing them first before trimming, as dirt will blunt the scissors. (See bathing instructions above.) Once they are totally dry (a dog dryer works wonders here!), you can start

Before & after trimming (UK style)

grooming. Using a grooming table makes it much easier to get to all the parts of the dog, though if you do use a table, make sure to never leave the dog unattended. Give your dog a good brush all over, gently brushing out any knots, especially the longer areas, like tail, back of legs, under ears and around the neck.

Grooming tools required

This photo shows some of the more common grooming tools. I would recommend having all of these.

- 🐾 Soft boar hair or nylon brush
- 🐾 Pin brush
- 🐾 Lawrence Tender Care slicker brush (square)
- 🐾 Metal comb
- 🐾 Nail trimmers (Millers Forge)
- 🐾 Straight-edged scissors (6–7 inch)
- 🐾 Double-sided thinning scissors (30–40 teeth)

Another useful tool is the Mars Coat King, which works well to thin hair out, especially around the neck.

Grooming tools can be purchased from many online pet stores. Scissors vary a lot in price and quality, but good scissors will last a lifetime. Wahl and Roseline brands offer good mid-range scissors.

Feet and nails

Golden Retriever feet are meant to be neat and cat-like. If left to grow, the hair will look like fluffy slippers and your dog will carry large amounts of dirt inside on their feet. If you keep their feet trimmed, you will get less dirt and wet paw prints.

Grooming can be done on a table, but my dogs are quite comfortable laying on the floor for me do their feet and nails.

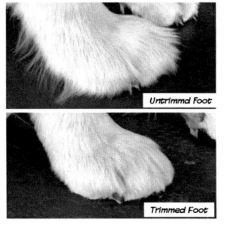

Untrimmed Foot

Trimmed Foot

The underside of the foot needs to be trimmed carefully around all the pads and nails need to be kept short. Don't forget to trim the dew claws! If your dog is on concrete regularly you may find their nails stay nice and short without the need for trimming, but don't assume this will be the case! Nails are often neglected, which can lead to foot problems. You can use nail clippers or a Dremel tool to trim the nails. Avoid cutting the quick (the blood vessels) in the nail, as this is very painful. (If you do accidentally cut it, dab with corn flour or a cake of soap to stop the bleeding.) If you are not confident trimming nails, ask your breeder or a groomer to do it for you.

Neck

Golden Retrievers grow a lot of thick hair around their neck. This "ruff" is loved by many, who like the lion look.

For showing in the UK, Australia, NZ, and Europe, we trim this hair out to give the neck more shape. It is also easier to care for if thinned out. But whether you do this comes down to your own personal preference.

Use thinning scissors to tidy the neck hair, always cutting upwards, and brush after every few cuts to remove cut hair.

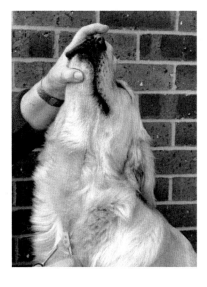

Ears

Start by cleaning the ears out with an ear cleaner. My preferred choice is Epi-Otic. Squirt the cleaner right into the ear canal so it is full of liquid and massage thoroughly (it will sound squelchy). Wipe out with cotton wool or swabs. (Never use cotton buds.)

Now you're ready to trim the ears.

The underside of the ears is prone to knots and can get matted. Start by thinning out this hair with the double-sided thinning scissors.

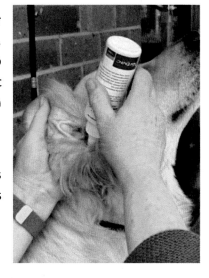

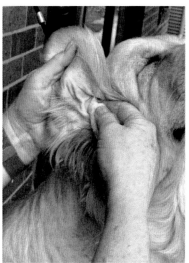

This not only prevents matting but also lets air get into the ears and keeps them dry, which can reduce ear infections.

Next, use the thinning scissors to trim off the fluffy long hair on the top of the ears for a neater look. Brush away the trimmed hair after each cut so you can see what you are doing.

Now use the sharp, straight-sided scissors to carefully trim around the ear flap.

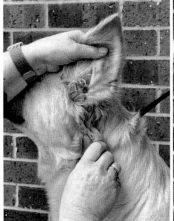  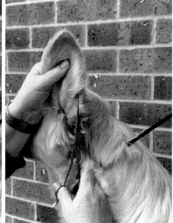 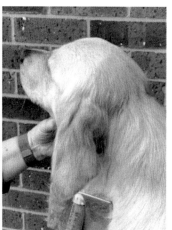

| *Step 1: Thin the underside* | *Step 2: Trim the upper side* | *Step 3: Trim around the flap* | *The finished result* |

Tail

This is a simple job, but one many people worry about doing. The tail is meant to be trimmed to just below the hock (ankle) joint. In most Goldens, if you run your hand down their tail towards the ground, you'll feel that the tail bone ends at around this level.

To trim the hair, grasp all the tail feathers, twist them, and hold them with your thumb over the end of the tail bone to make sure you don't cut it. Trim off all the excess hair 1 cm below the end of the bone.

Now release the hair, hold the tail out, and brush the hair down. You can then shape the hair with your straight scissors, trimming off small amounts at a time until you get the shape and length you want, aiming for a lovely fan shape.

Some people love a long fluffy tail and do not want to trim it. Obviously, this is personal choice, but leaving very long hair requires more grooming as the tail tends to collect sticks and dirt.

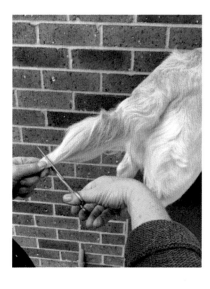  

Hind legs and feet

The photos on the right show before, during, and after trimming of the hind feet.

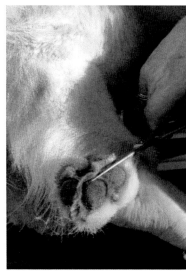

The front feet are trimmed in the same way as the hind feet, by carefully cutting around the edges and then cutting the long hair around and between the pads on the underside.

The long hair on the back of the lower leg can be trimmed off using the thinning scissors to give a nice, neat look.

Teeth

Your grooming routine should include checking your dog's teeth. Make sure they are nice and white, not broken or chipped, and if you have a puppy, check that the adult teeth seem to be coming through normally, with no retained baby teeth (which you can see as two teeth trying to occupy the same space). The most common dental problem in older dogs is tartar, which usually starts on the rear molars as yellowish stains and gets worse over time. As it builds up, it can cause gum disease and bacterial infections. Surprisingly, many people never look at their dog's teeth and are quite shocked when they are told their dog has a dental problem.

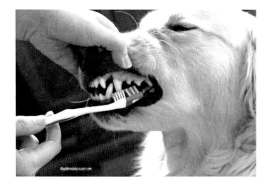

Get your puppy used to having their teeth checked, and buy a soft dog toothbrush and dog toothpaste to clean them. (Never use human toothpaste.) You can also add a dried seaweed meal powder such as Plaque Off to their diet to help control bacteria in the mouth and reduce buildup of tartar. My own dogs get regular raw meaty bones which help keep their teeth in great condition.

Disclaimer: I am not a vet, but I have worked as a vet nurse and in the veterinary industry for over 30 years. If you have any concerns about your dog's health you should always contact your veterinary surgeon for advice.

Below are a few products used to treat common health conditions in Australia. These, or equivalent products depending on your location, are handy to have in your **medicine cupboard**. The products are discussed below in the relevant sections.

For skin and ears:
- Wound-Gard spray
- Curash powder (for hot spots)
- Epi-Otic ear cleaner
- Medicated shampoo
- 5% hydrogen peroxide
- Betadine (disinfectant)
- Colloidal silver
- Vet wrap (self-adhesive bandage)
- Gauze swabs
- Saline for flushing
- 10 & 20 mL syringes

For gut upsets:
- Pro-Kolin+ paste
- ProN8ure probiotic
- Slippery Elm powder
- Lectade electrolyte powder

General:
- Digital thermometer
- Non-latex gloves
- Tick removal tool

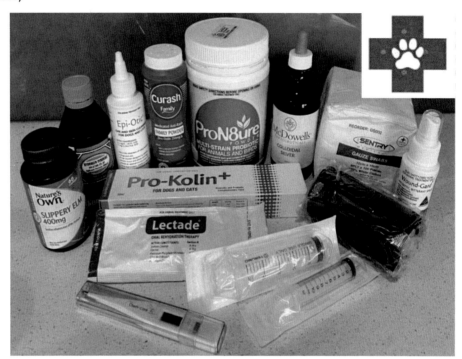

Fleas, Ticks, and Other Creepy Things

Fleas

In most dogs, flea bites cause an allergic reaction in the skin that can be intensely itchy and lead to severe scratching. Fleas can also spread tapeworm, and heavy burdens can lead to anaemia (low red blood cell count). Fleas do not just live on your dog. Fleas and their eggs and larvae live everywhere in your dog's environment, including their bedding, your carpet, and the soil outside. A flea infestation therefore requires quite some effort to control, so prevention is a much wiser strategy.

There are many effective flea treatments on the market, including chews and topical spot-on preparations. Many "all-in-one" products (e.g. Advocate, Comfortis Plus, Sentinel Spectra, Nexgard Spectra) are now available that also control intestinal worms and heartworm. (Note, however, that most products do not include tapeworm.) Older products such as flea collars, sprays, powders, and baths are far less effective and should be avoided. Consult your vet on the different products available.

If you do have a flea problem, you will also need to treat the whole house and outside if you want to eliminate all the eggs and larvae.

Heartworm

Heartworm is spread by mosquitoes and its prevalence is therefore higher in warm, humid climates. Heartworms develop into large, spaghetti-like adult worms that live in the heart. Infection can be life-threatening, depending on how far the disease has progressed, and treatment is difficult and fraught with risk.

Heartworm disease can easily be prevented. Preventative treatment options include an annual injection (Proheart), monthly chews, and topical products. Many of the new combined flea/worm chews and spot-ons cover heartworm. You should consult with your vet about the most suitable treatment for your dog, and when treatment should begin. If your dog is older than 6 months and has not been on preventative treatment, they may require a blood test to check for existing heartworm infection before preventative treatment can be started.

Ticks

Ticks are a worldwide problem and occur in most countries. Ticks are renowned for transmitting many serious diseases to dogs, including Lyme disease, ehrlichiosis, babesiosis, Rocky Mountain spotted fever, and many more.

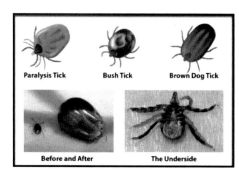

In Australia we have several varieties of ticks, but the one of most concern is the paralysis tick, which is found along the eastern coast of Australia. This tick causes sudden paralysis and quickly progresses to death as the breathing muscles stop working. Each year many dogs and cats lose their lives to this tick. Thankfully, there are now new highly effective, long-acting tick prevention products on the market, some of which include worm and flea treatment as well.

Prevention is available in several forms, including oral chews, long-acting collars, and spot-ons. The new-generation products such as Bravecto, Nexgard, and Simparica are highly effective. However, some of these products can cause side effects and are not without risk, so discuss this with your veterinarian before choosing a product.

Skin, Ears, and Anal Glands

Hot spots (moist superficial dermatitis)

A hot spot is a surface-level skin infection. It can appear and spread very quickly, often appearing overnight and growing from a coin-sized pink spot to a large, red, raw, oozing sore in a matter of hours. Hot spots occur when the surface of the skin becomes moist and warm, creating the right conditions for bacteria to overgrow.

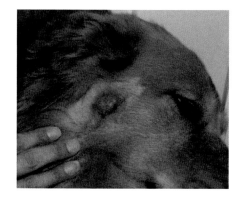

Hot spots are most common in areas without good air flow, such as under the collar and around the ears. They often result from licking and scratching, or insufficient drying after swimming or bathing.

A single flea bite or scratch of a sore ear can be enough to cause a hot spot. If left unchecked, the sore can become large and painful, and the deeper layers of the skin can get infected. The worse it gets, the itchier it gets. The dog then does more damage by scratching, leading to a vicious cycle.

If you catch a hot spot early, you can try to treat it yourself. Bathe the area once or twice a day with a gentle antibacterial wash like Betadine or chlorhexidine, then dry it thoroughly. An excellent shampoo to have on hand is Malaseb, which is antibacterial and can sometimes stop an infection in its tracks. If the hot spot is in an area where your dog can chew at it, a great option is the antiseptic spray Wound-gard, which also contains a bitterant to deter licking and chewing. Some people have great success using colloidal silver ointment on small hot spots. Curash powder can be helpful to relieve itch and dry the area.

If you find a more serious hot spot, or if a hot spot is worsening despite the above interventions, it will need veterinary attention. If the lesion is larger than a 20-cent piece or there are multiple hot spots, your vet may prescribe antibiotics, anti-inflammatories, and possibly additional pain relief. Normally the infected area is shaved to keep it cool and dry. If the sore is on the head, you may need to use a plastic head cone or soft collar to protect the area.

As with anything, prevention is always better than cure. Anything you can do to prevent moist, warm conditions at the surface of the skin will reduce the risk of hot spots. Always make sure your dog is completely dry after swimming or bathing, particularly in skin folds and areas without good air flow. Take off collars and harnesses when you are at home and they are not needed. Maintain good grooming practices. And always use a good-quality flea prevention product.

Puppy Pyoderma

Pyoderma is a bacterial infection of the skin that can affect all ages, but is most common in puppies. It affects deeper skin layers than a hot spot, and tends not to be as localised. Often it appears as small, red, pimple-like bumps on the skin. The spots may just look like little pink spots, or there may be visible pustules, similar to human pimples. You might also notice flaky or scaly rings of dry skin, which are old pustules that have started to heal.

The most common places to see signs of puppy pyoderma are on the belly and in the groin or armpits, where the fur is sparse. Sometimes pyoderma causes itchiness, but this is usually mild. Most puppies show no sign of being irritated, itchy, or in pain. They usually remain well and continue to eat, drink, and behave normally. You can bathe the area with salty water or use a medicated antibacterial shampoo, and it will usually clear up quickly.

Puppy Warts (Canine Papillomavirus)

Wart-like lesions around or in the mouth and face region of puppies are called papillomas, and are usually due to the canine papillomavirus. Papillomas are quite common in puppies and are generally harmless. In most cases they disappear or drop off over 2–3 months and don't require treatment. However, occasionally a puppy will have many warts and may require veterinary treatment.

The important thing to remember is that while the lesions are present, the puppies are potentially shedding the papillomavirus. The virus is quite contagious, so when puppies play together, mouthing each other, playing with each other's toys, or sharing water bowls, the disease is spread. Once the lesions clear up, the virus is no longer being shed.

Allergies

Allergies (skin, respiratory, or gut) are quite common in dogs and are often difficult to definitively diagnose. Environmental allergens may come from many things in the environment, including plants, grasses, food, household chemicals, dust mites, or flea bites.

Dogs with allergies may show the following symptoms:

- Chewing the feet or legs
- Scratching the body
- Recurrent ear infections
- Sneezing, runny eyes and nose
- Gastrointestinal upsets
- Hair loss
- Itchy, red skin

Veterinary dermatologists can do certain tests to help determine the cause of an allergy, but as with human allergies, there can be multiple factors at play and the process can be lengthy, expensive, and sometimes unrewarding. It is common to treat the allergies without necessarily identifying exactly what is causing them.

Allergies are sometimes treated with antihistamines, which are a good initial option as they are inexpensive, safe, and can be used long term. Some of the common human brands may be used, but only under veterinary supervision. For many dogs, though, antihistamines are not very effective. In the past, steroids were the only other option for controlling itch, but today there are much safer medications for treating allergies.

True food allergies in dogs are quite rare; they are thought to account for only about 1% of itchy dogs. The most common cause of food allergies is red-meat protein. Grain allergy is extremely rare in dogs. Food allergies are usually diagnosed by doing an "elimination diet" under veterinary supervision. You may have to try several diets under veterinary recommendation before you work out the best one for your dog. The most important thing is to avoid any food or treat that you have identified as a trigger. Today there are many excellent single-protein meal options, such as the Prime range of rolls in Australia, which are sold by many vets and pet stores.

Many vets recommend adding an omega-3 and -6 supplement to meals to keep the skin and coat healthy. Dogs with mild allergies often respond well to these.

Ear infections

Ear infections in Golden Retrievers are not uncommon, partly because they love swimming and have floppy ears. When water gets into the ear canal there is limited air flow to help it dry out, making for a moist, warm environment that is ideal for bacteria and yeast to overgrow. Rarely, an ear infection can be the result of food allergies or a foreign body such as a grass seed. The most common symptoms are scratching at the ear and shaking the head.

Check your dog's ears weekly for brown or black discharge, or a yeasty smell. Any sign of pain, redness, discharge, or inflammation requires a vet visit. Treatment is likely to include antibiotic/antifungal ear drops, and in serious cases sedation and an ear flush. Ear infections can be difficult to treat.

Preventing ear infections is a matter of avoiding the moist, warm conditions that lead to ear infections. If your dog swims often, clean the ears out using a product like Epi-Otic or Otoflush, which are designed to have a drying effect. When you bathe your dog, avoid getting water in the ears.

Anal glands

These innocuous little glands that sit under the tail go unnoticed by most people… until the dog releases them! Then you get a pungent, fishy smell coming from their back end. You may notice some yellow/brown liquid. Normally the glands release a small amount of fluid to provide lubrication when your dog passes a stool, but they can get released in larger amounts when a dog is stressed or gets a fright.

It is not uncommon for these glands get inflamed or blocked. When this happens, you will see your dog dragging their bottom along the ground. You may need to visit the vet to get them emptied. Anal glands are best left alone unless there is a problem; often we find that the more they get emptied, the more they need to be emptied. Each time the glands are expressed it may cause irritation in the area, which can lead to infection. If your dog has problems with the anal glands, adding fibre, such as Metamucil, to the diet daily may help.

Insect stings

Insect stings and bites are quite common, especially in puppies, whose natural curiosity leads them to investigate bees, wasps, spiders, ants, and anything else they can find! Symptoms of a bite or sting can be dramatic: they can become very itchy, their face may swell, and in severe cases the whole head becomes swollen. If that swelling spreads to the throat, they may collapse and struggle to breathe. This is a medical emergency, so contact your vet immediately. Anaphylaxis can occur in rare cases.

If you think your puppy may be having an allergic reaction, contact your vet immediately for treatment advice. They will likely ask you to come to the clinic for an antihistamine injection.

Grass seeds

Every summer vets are kept busy removing grass seeds from dogs' feet, eyes, ears, and other body parts. If you have a long-coated dog like a Golden Retriever and they have access to long, dry grass, you need to check their feet (especially between the toes), eyes, and ears daily.

Grass seeds can migrate right into the body of the dog and cause serious, sometimes life-threatening problems. In summer, avoid long, dry grass and keep your Golden's feet trimmed. The first sign of a grass seed starting to migrate through the skin is usually incessant licking, redness, and swelling. Often sedation and surgery are required to remove the seeds and antibiotics may be prescribed for infection.

Vomiting and diarrhoea

Gastrointestinal upsets are quite common in puppies and adult dogs. Common causes include change in diet, stress, or eating something they shouldn't. Infections (bacteria, viruses, parasites, and protozoa) can also be involved.

If your puppy has vomiting or diarrhoea, contact your vet for advice. Often they will ask you to come to the clinic for an appointment. Puppies can get dehydrated quickly, and vomiting and diarrhoea can quickly become serious.

In mild cases, you may be able to manage the problem at home, and your vet will offer guidance on what to do. Usually this involves withholding food for 8–12 hours and offer fresh water, then, if they are bright and not vomiting, feeding a bland diet that is gentle on the stomach.

A good "bland diet" consists of boiled turkey or chicken breast shredded and mixed with boiled or canned mashed pumpkin (mashed pumpkin is now regarded as a better option than boiled rice). Start with 1 tablespoon four times daily. If this is tolerated well, you can add some boiled brown rice to the mix after a few days.

A **probiotic** powder such as ProN8ure or paste such as Protexin Pro-Kolin+ are excellent products to keep handy in the fridge for any upset tummies and will help in many simple cases. **Slippery Elm powder** is also very good for soothing the gut (you can pull a capsule apart and sprinkle it on food). Mix these in with the bland diet.

After 48 hours, if the puppy is doing well, add ¼ cup of dry kibble (ideally a sensitive stomach variety) to the chicken/pumpkin/rice mix. Over the next few days, gradually increase the kibble and reintroduce any meat until you are back to normal quantities.

Any puppy or dog that has continual vomiting or diarrhoea; seems genuinely unwell, depressed, or weak; or is passing blood needs to be seen by a vet urgently.

Medical Emergencies – Snake Bites, Poisoning, Heat Stroke

Snake bites

Every year many dogs lose their lives to snake bites. Many of those dogs are Golden Retrievers. Being a hunting breed, Goldens love to chase most things that move, including lizards and snakes.

Signs of snake bite include weakness, vomiting, collapse, bleeding, dilated pupils, drooling, and panting. Some types of snake bite can potentially be fatal if not treated promptly.

A snake bite is an emergency and time is critical. If you suspect your dog may have been bitten, keep them as quiet as possible, phone your vet, and take them straight in. If possible, carry your dog to the car to limit movement. Depending on your location and how confident you are that it is a snake bite, you may wish to go straight to an emergency clinic, since many general practice clinics will not stock antivenom. If a limb has been bitten you can apply a pressure bandage, but in most cases, bites are on the face.

If you have the opportunity, take a photo of the snake to help with identification. The most common snake bites in Australia are from tiger, eastern brown, copperhead, and red-bellied black snakes. In the UK and Europe, they have the adder, in North America the rattlesnake, in Asia the cobra, and there are many other snake species in other countries.

Poisons

There are far too many poisons to list here, but you will find a **poisonous plant list** in Appendix 1 at the back of this book. The safest approach is to treat every plant as potentially poisonous.

The most common (and some of the most dangerous) household poisons are rat bait and snail bait. Other common poisons are chocolate, xylitol (artificial sweetener), onions (including garlic and leek), grapes (and raisins and sultanas), antifreeze, ant bait, fertilisers, household chemicals, and human medicines.

Snail bait should just never be used in any garden with pets. It is often fatal if ingested and is very tasty to dogs. It is a truly awful way for a pet to die.

Rat bait poisoning is quite common in autumn, and may present with bleeding from the gums or eyes, blood in the stools, pale gums, weakness, and/or bruising on the body. If caught early, it can be treated. Unfortunately, dogs seem quite partial to eating rat bait, or even dead rats or mice that have been poisoned. You may be unaware if they have eaten a poisoned rodent, as your neighbour may have used baits.

If you suspect your pet has eaten something poisonous, do not wait and see. Call the vet immediately and be ready to tell them exactly what you think they may have eaten. If caught early, a vet may be able to make a dog vomit to bring up the poison.

Heat stroke

Australia and many other countries can be extremely hot in summer, and sadly every year many dogs die due to heat stroke. No dog should ever be left in a car, even for short periods. Dogs can also get heat stroke from lack of shade or being exercised in hot weather, especially in high humidity.

Symptoms of heat stroke include panting, collapse, salivation, and blue gums. This is an emergency. Apply cool wet towels over the dog's legs to help them cool down, and get to a vet urgently. Do not use ice-cold water or ice packs, as this can cause the body to try to conserve heat and make things worse.

In summer months, only walk your puppy or adult at cooler times of day. Exercise caution whenever the temperature is over 25 degrees. Avoid hot roads or footpaths, as they can burn feet. Always carry fresh water when exercising your dog.

As much fun as swimming can be, avoid the temptation to drag your dog to the beach on a 40-degree day. Golden Retrievers are not designed for extreme heat, and subjecting them to very hot temperatures is dangerous. On a hot day they are much happier sitting at home in the air conditioning, or in their own paddling pool.

Foreign body ingestion

Puppies love to chew, and sometimes they also decide to swallow things they shouldn't. Socks, stones, corn cobs, and children's small toys are among their favourites. If you see your puppy swallow something like a sock or toy, a quick trip to the vet now can often save you from awfully expensive and risky surgery later. If a foreign body gets stuck, the only way out is with surgery. Corn cobs are notorious for this, due to their roughness and shape. Surprisingly, socks do sometimes pass through – but don't assume they will!

A bowel obstruction is a very serious medical emergency. Symptoms of obstruction can include vomiting, not eating, lethargy, a sore belly, and struggling to pass poo. X-rays are usually the first step to work out whether there is an obstruction, though this won't always give a definitive diagnosis. Sometimes the only way to be sure whether there is an obstruction is with surgery.

If you witness your dog swallowing or eating something they shouldn't, your vet can make them vomit by giving them a drug to induce vomiting. It is important that you get your dog to the vet straight away; do not wait even for a few hours or it will be too late. Call your vet immediately.

Bloat (GDV)

Gastric dilatation-volvulus (GDV), commonly referred to as "bloat", is a very serious condition that can be fatal if left untreated – and sometimes even when it is treated. GDV occurs when a dog's stomach fills with gas, food, or fluid and subsequently twists on itself. GDV develops without warning and can progress quickly. It is always an emergency.

Symptoms of bloat include a swollen and painful belly, retching without vomiting, drooling, groaning, and other signs of distress such as panting and restlessness. Call your vet immediately if you suspect bloat, as every minute without treatment increases the risk of further damage and potentially death.

Joint Disease and Arthritis

Cruciate ligament disease

You may know the cruciate ligament as the one in the knee that many footballers tear. While footballers usually injure it in one fell swoop, in dogs cruciate injuries are usually thought to be related to repetitive strain on the ligament due to high-impact activities such as ball fetching and running on hard surfaces such as sand.

A dog that has torn their cruciate ligament will often suddenly go lame. They might give out a sudden yelp and hold their hind leg up. This often happens after a sudden twist, or when they are running fast.

If you suspect your dog may have torn their cruciate ligament, you will need to see your vet to get a diagnosis and work out the best treatment option. There are a few different surgical options, but the TPLO (tibial plateau levelling osteotomy) is regarded as the gold standard and is a far superior option for large-breed dogs. This usually costs thousands of dollars and involves 12–16 weeks of recovery and rehabilitation. As in humans, great care must be taken to build the strength back up. Unfortunately, it is not unusual for the other knee to rupture within 12 months, so be prepared!

Prevention of cruciate disease is about avoiding predisposing factors and being sensible with exercise. There is strong evidence that desexing at an early age increases the risk of cruciate ligament disease, and overweight dogs are also far more susceptible to this injury. Just like us, dogs need to work up to hard exercise and need a warmup. On hard surfaces such as sand, it's safest to avoid jumping and hard running. Swimming is an excellent no-impact exercise option that puts no strain on the knees at all.

Arthritis

Arthritis means inflammation of the joints, and unfortunately it is an inevitable part of aging. Dogs with poorly conformed joints (this shouldn't apply to your puppy if you've chosen a good breeder!) or that have had a previous joint injury may develop arthritis at a younger age. Arthritis is progressive, and will always get worse over time.

Signs of arthritis may include limping/lameness; reluctance to walk, climb stairs, or play; lagging on walks; difficulty getting up; and licking affected joints.

If your puppy or adult is diagnosed with arthritis, the pain can be greatly alleviated by making sure your dog is a healthy weight; providing regular, gentle exercise and a warm bed; and using natural supplements such as fish oil, Antinol Rapid, Rosehip Vital Canine, YuMOVE, 4 Cyte, and/or hemp oil. There are also some excellent veterinary diets and injectable drugs that can provide good relief and support for the joints.

As arthritis progresses, your vet may recommend acupuncture, oral medication, and/or referral to a specialist. More serious joint disease sometimes requires surgery. As in human medicine, new products for arthritis are always being launched and some look very promising. Ask your vet for more information.

To support the joints and delay the onset of arthritis as they get older, all puppies can be started on an omega-3 fish oil supplement from puppyhood. This will benefit not just their joints but also their skin. You can use 1000 mg human fish oil capsules, or you can use an omega-3 supplement specifically for dogs.

Cancer

Unfortunately, Golden Retrievers are more prone to cancer than some other breeds. In young dogs the most common cancers are the "mast cell tumour" (a skin cancer) and lymphoma (cancer of the lymph nodes).

In older dogs, one of the most common cancers in Golden Retrievers is "haemangiosarcoma" (cancer of the blood vessels). This cancer can be quite devastating. An apparently healthy dog can suddenly become unwell and die quickly when a previously unidentified tumour on the spleen or liver ruptures. Other common cancers in middle-aged and older dogs include "osteosarcoma" (cancer of the bone) and melanoma, which can form on the skin or in the mouth.

As in humans, cancer seems to be on the rise in dogs, too. Any lump or bump on your dog should always be checked by your vet. Many cancers can be successfully treated if caught early. In an older dog, annual checkups are a must, and any signs of slowing down, pain, lumps, or a bloated belly should be investigated. Research shows that, as in humans, there is a close correlation between lifestyle and cancer. Passive smoking and exposure to herbicides, pesticides, and other carcinogenic chemicals can reduce your dog's lifespan.

HEREDITARY CONDITIONS AND TESTING

The Golden Retriever is regarded as a relatively healthy breed, but as with most dog breeds it does have some genetic disorders which you should be aware of before purchasing a puppy. Responsible breeders will do health testing and screening to ensure you receive a healthy puppy and to reduce the occurrence of these conditions in the breed.

Below are the **four types of testing a responsible breeder should do** on all breeding stock before breeding:

- Hip and elbow scoring using an accepted grading system
- An annual eye certificate from a veterinary ophthalmologist
- A heart certificate from a veterinary cardiologist
- DNA testing – In Australia a full profile includes testing for the following diseases: degenerative myelopathy, dystrophic epidermolysis bullosa (Golden Retriever type), generalised PRA 1 (Golden Retriever type), generalised PRA 2 (Golden Retriever type), ichthyosis A (Golden Retriever type), osteogenesis imperfecta (Golden Retriever type), progressive rod cone degeneration (PRCD), skeletal dysplasia 2 (mild disproportionate dwarfism). In other countries, slightly different profiles may be available.

DNA testing

Responsible breeders now get their dogs and puppies DNA tested. In the future this may become compulsory for registered breeders. DNA samples can only be collected by an approved DNA collector, which may be a vet or another qualified person. The dog's identity is verified (usually by microchip) and a cheek swab or blood sample is taken (they are equally accurate). The sample is carefully placed in a sterile packet, labelled, and sent to a laboratory. The breeder will then get the results back in several weeks. Worldwide, the most common diseases tested for in Golden Retrievers are progressive retinal atrophy, ichthyosis, degenerative myelopathy, Muscular Dystrophy, and neuronal ceroid lipofuscinosis. Currently there are no DNA tests for hip dysplasia, elbow dysplasia, or cataracts, although scientists are working on this for the future.

Hip Dysplasia

Golden Retrievers are susceptible to hip dysplasia, an inherited instability of the hip joints. This instability can be compounded by various factors, such as overexercising, overfeeding and the associated rapid growth in puppies, and early desexing. Hip dysplasia is a multifactorial disease caused by multiple genes combined with environmental factors, and eliminating it from the breed is far from straightforward.

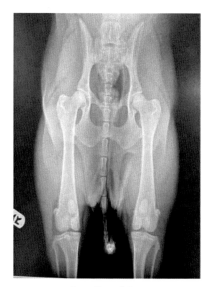

Excellent hips

Currently, Australian breeders use the ANKC's Canine Hip and Elbow Dysplasia Scheme (CHEDS) to assess the degree of hip dysplasia a dog has. Other systems are used internationally, including the BVA scheme in the UK, the OFA scheme in the USA, the FCI scheme in Europe, and the SV scheme in Germany.

Under CHEDS, dogs are X-rayed after 12 months of age and the hips are scored by a specialist. Each hip joint is given a score between 0 and 53 and these are added to give a total score, e.g. 5:9 (14). The lower the score the better the hips; a dog with two perfect hips has a score of 0:0 (0). Other schemes take a different tack; for example, under the OFA scheme, X-rays are taken at age 2 and hips are classified as Excellent, Good, Fair, Borderline, Mild, Moderate, or Severe.

Very few Golden Retrievers have perfect hips. A slight irregularity in the ball or socket may give a CHEDS score of, for example, 2:3 (5). The more irregular the ball and socket are, the higher the score. Golden Retrievers with high hip scores should not be used for breeding.

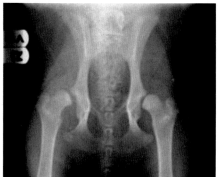

Extremely poor hips (note lack of sockets)

There are multiple databases worldwide that keep records of all scores and calculates the breed average. At 1 January 2023 in Australia the average total was 10.49, and the median was 8. These scores are calculated from the X-rays submitted to the scheme, which reflects only a small proportion of the total Golden Retriever population. The overall average is likely much higher.

The only way hip dysplasia can be diagnosed is by X-ray. Some dogs may have terrible hips yet not show any symptoms until older. Therefore, all potential breeding dogs must be screened by X-ray.

PennHip

Another method used to assess hips is called PennHIP (University of Pennsylvania Hip Improvement Program). Under this system, hips can be assessed from 16 weeks of age. This is a scientific method to evaluate a dog for its susceptibility to osteoarthritis resulting from hip dysplasia. The radiographic procedure involves a special positioning of the dog so that the dog's "passive hip laxity" can be accurately measured. In simple terms, passive hip laxity refers to the degree of looseness of the ball in the hip socket when the dog's muscles are completely relaxed. The dog must be fully anesthetised, and three different X-rays are taken. PennHip radiographs are better at detecting hip dysplasia than the more popular UK and OFA schemes.

Elbow Dysplasia

"Elbow dysplasia" is a term used to describe one or more inherited developmental abnormalities in a dog's elbow joint, which lead to arthritis in the elbow joint.

Golden Retrievers are susceptible to elbow dysplasia, and Australian breeders screen their dogs under the CHEDS scheme. A dog's elbows are X-rayed when they are over 12 months of age and the X-rays are scored from 0 to 3 by a specialist, with 0 being normal and 3 being severely affected. As with hip dysplasia, there are several different grading schemes used worldwide.

A dog with elbow dysplasia may have intermittent lameness or be very sore. In serious cases, surgery is the only option to reduce the pain.

The CHEDS score sheet used by ANKC Australia for hip and elbow results

Eye Diseases

Golden Retrievers can suffer from several genetic eye problems, including progressive retinal atrophy (PRA), hereditary cataracts, and multifocal retinal dysplasia. Breeders worldwide screen their dogs for these eye conditions, and in Australia breeders are expected to screen annually. ACES (Australian Canine Eye Scheme) eye certificates are stored in a national database known as ORCHID. As with hips and elbows, there are different databases worldwide, e.g. in the USA it is the Companion Animal Eye Registry (CAER).

Cataracts

A cataract is an opacity in the eye lens. There are many causes of cataracts, but some are inherited. If cataracts are in both eyes, the dog may eventually become blind. Surgery is available in these cases, though this is very expensive. The most common cataract in Golden Retrievers is the "posterior, polar, subcapsular (PPS) cataract", better known as the star cataract. It is usually in both eyes and often becomes apparent at 6–18 months of age, though it can appear as late as 6–7 years of age or as early as 6–8 weeks. These cataracts may be slowly progressive, but rarely interfere with vision. The condition is inherited, so it is advisable not to breed from affected animals.

Multifocal retinal dysplasia (MRD)

Multifocal retinal dysplasia is a condition where the retina develops abnormally, resulting in "folds" in the normally flat surface of the retina at the back of the eye. There are various causes for retinal dysplasia, but most commonly it is inherited. It is seen in several breeds, including the Golden Retriever, and does not normally affect

The ACES eye certificate (AU)

vision. Most commonly it is found when a veterinary ophthalmologist is examining breeding dogs prior to breeding as part of the Australian Canine Eye Scheme (ACES).

Progressive retinal atrophy (PRA)

Progressive retinal atrophy is a group of inherited genetic diseases where the retina degenerates, causing vision loss. Affected dogs initially show signs of night blindness, but over time day vision degenerates as well, until eventually vision is lost completely. Most dogs with PRA also end up developing cataracts. PRA is inherited as an "autosomal recessive" trait, which means that a dog can carry the gene without being affected, and both parents must be affected for the disease to be passed on. DNA tests are available for three PRA genes: prcd-PRA, GR_PRA1 and GR_PRA2. This condition is rare in Australian Golden Retrievers.

Entropion

Entropion is an inherited condition of the eyelid where the border of the eyelid turns in and hair on the outside of the lid rubs on the cornea (surface of the eye). This causes irritation and, in severe cases, ulceration of the cornea. Surgery is required to alleviate discomfort and prevent damage to the eye. This is normally performed when the dog is a puppy. Affected animals should not be used in a breeding program.

Distichia (extra eyelashes)

Distichia (extra eyelashes) grow from glands right on the eyelid edge, forming a second row of eyelashes. Extra eyelashes may or may not cause irritation to the eye. This condition will be noted on an eye certificate, but most Golden Retrievers that are affected do not have evidence of corneal irritation and do not require any kind of intervention.

Glaucoma

Glaucoma is caused by increased pressure within the eye. This increased pressure can rapidly cause blindness and pain. It is hard to assess pain in animals, but we know it is painful in humans, and vets find that nearly all their patients are brighter and more active after having glaucoma relieved. Humans describe the pain as being like a bad headache; you can function, but not happily. Unfortunately, many dogs with glaucoma ultimately need the affected eye(s) removed.

Normally, the eye is in a constant balance between production and drainage of fluid. In "primary" glaucoma, the outflow of fluid from the eye is blocked by an abnormal "drainage angle". In "secondary" glaucoma, the drainage angle becomes blocked due to inflammation, lens luxation, blood in the eye, or growths inside the eye. Golden Retrievers are prone to primary glaucoma, and many breeders now get drainage angles checked and graded in their breeding animals.

Golden Retriever pigmentary uveitis (GRPU)

Pigmentary uveitis (GRPU) is a condition where pigment is laid down on the capsule of the lens, which ultimately leads to glaucoma and blindness. It was first recognised in Golden Retrievers in the late 1990s in dogs living in the north-eastern region of Golden Retriever the United States. Since these first reports, the disease has been seen in Golden Retrievers across the United States and Canada, with an estimated prevalence of 5–10%. It is uncommon in Golden Retrievers outside of these regions. Most dogs diagnosed are over the age of 5 years, and the average age at the time of diagnosis is 8–10 years old. GRPU is considered an inherited disease; however, the pattern of inheritance and underlying genetics remain unknown and there is currently no DNA test or effective long-term treatment. There is a lot of research being carried out on this condition, so hopefully this will change in future.

Heart Conditions

Hereditary heart disease is another concern in Golden Retrievers, with the main condition being subaortic stenosis (SAS). Dogs with SAS may faint or even collapse and die, but in mild cases they often live a relatively normal life. It is the responsibility of the breeder to never breed any dog with a heritable heart condition. Reputable breeders get all breeding stock heart tested after 12 months of age by a veterinary cardiologist, who will certify that the dog has no evidence of heart disease.

Recently Golden Retrievers have started to be diagnosed with dilated cardiomyopathy (DCM), a condition they are not usually predisposed to. This condition has been associated with feeding of grain-free, boutique-style food with high percentages of peas and lentils. This type of diet should therefore be avoided in Golden Retrievers.

Other Inherited Health Conditions

Ichthyosis (ICTH)

Ichthyosis is an inherited skin condition that occurs in many breeds of dogs, as well as in humans. The name derives from the Greek word for "fish", which relates to the appearance and quality of the skin: Dogs with ichthyosis may develop flaky skin, which can sometimes blacken and become dry and rough but is not usually itchy.

Ichthyosis is a lifelong condition, but in the Golden Retriever it is usually self-limiting, with most dogs suffering no more than dandruff-like flaking. Some affected dogs only show signs in times of stress, some show no signs at all, and some are affected only as puppies. Feeding a diet rich in omega-3 and -6 oils, regular grooming with a rubber brush, and bathing in oatmeal shampoos can help.

Ichthyosis is inherited as an "autosomal recessive" trait, which means a dog must have two copies (one from each parent) of the mutated gene to be affected. Recently a more severe form of ichthyosis has been identified in Golden Retrievers, and a new DNA test is available.

Epilepsy

Golden Retrievers, like many other breeds, can develop idiopathic epilepsy ("idiopathic" means there is no known cause). This is strongly suspected to be hereditary, though the mode of inheritance is unknown. No dog with epilepsy should not be used for breeding. It is worth asking any potential breeder if their lines have it.

The symptoms of canine epilepsy are seizures. These can range from mild and almost unnoticeable to full "grand-mal" seizures, which are very scary to witness. The dog may stiffen, fall over, and convulse, and may urinate and defecate. Do not attempt to stop a seizure. Try to stay calm, and remove any items that may cause physical injury. The dog will be very disorientated and tired when they gain consciousness, and may not be themselves for a day or so.

If you dog has a seizure, the vet will likely ask questions and recommend tests to determine the cause, as seizures are not always related to epilepsy. They can occur after exposure to toxins and viral infections, as a result of disease, or as a result of injury. In these cases, once the dog is treated the seizures will usually cease. In older dogs, sudden-onset seizures may be caused by serious conditions such as brain tumours. If a thorough medical investigation cannot establish a cause, the diagnosis is idiopathic epilepsy.

Dogs with idiopathic epilepsy usually experience their first seizure between one and five years of age. A dog who has more than one seizure per month is usually treated with anticonvulsant drugs. These drugs are not a cure but an aid to reduce the frequency and severity of the seizures. Most dogs on these drugs can live a relatively normal life. There is some exciting research being done on epilepsy and using diet to reduce the incidence of seizures.

Ectopic ureter

Ectopic ureter ("wet puppy syndrome") is a condition where one or both ureters (the tube that connects the kidney to the bladder) does not enter the bladder in the correct position. Instead, it may open into the vagina, uterus, or urethra, causing constantly dribbling urine. This condition is sometimes seen in Golden Retrievers, more commonly in female puppies.

Puppies with ectopic ureter present with dripping urine, chronic urinary infections, a constantly wet bottom, and/or staining and scalding of the inside of their hind legs. Owners may notice the bedding is always wet.

Unfortunately, despite much research, the mode of inheritance of ectopic ureter has not been identified and there is no screening test. More genetic research is currently being undertaken in several countries. Sadly, breeders may humanely euthanise a puppy if this condition is detected when a puppy is very young. Surgery can be attempted to divert the ureters back into the bladder, but this operation is complex and expensive and may not be successful. Recently there has been some success using laser surgery.

Portosystemic (liver) shunt

A liver shunt is a congenital defect in the blood supply in the liver. At birth, a particular blood vessel is supposed to close in order to allow the puppy's liver to take over the work of cleaning the blood. If this does not occur it creates what's known as a "portosystemic shunt", which allows toxins to bypass the liver and makes the puppy unwell.

Symptoms may include poor coat, small size, vomiting and diarrhoea, sleepiness, lack of energy, and even seizures. Symptoms can be worse straight after a puppy has eaten. Specialist surgery is required to treat this condition and can be very complex depending on the location of the shunt. In some cases, surgery is just not possible, and euthanasia may be recommended. In mild cases, symptoms may not appear until the dog is older and the disease may even be manageable using a special diet and medications.

Hypothyroidism

Hypothyroidism is a condition where insufficient thyroid hormone is produced by the thyroid gland. Hypothyroidism causes a variety of symptoms but the most common are weight gain or obesity, hair loss, skin problems (dry, black skin flakes), and intolerance of the cold. Low thyroid levels are easy to detect with a blood test, though they are not always due to hypothyroidism, so the vet must interpret this finding in combination with the dog's symptoms, history, and other test results. Most dogs respond well to treatment with synthetic thyroid medication. Hypothyroidism most commonly develops in medium- to large-breed dogs between the ages of four and ten years. Some breeds, including the Golden Retriever, appear to be predisposed to this condition.

I love old dogs; they are so incredibly special and have such an air of wisdom in their eyes. With age, they do slow down, but they still enjoy life and we as owners need to make sure they are pain free and happy. They need a nice, warm, comfortable bed for achy bones; plenty of sleep time; and slower walks over a shorter distance. Walks are especially important for mental health and wellbeing, and to maintain muscle strength to support aging joints. Some dogs may require assistance or a ramp to get up the stairs or into the car, as they may not be able to jump up.

Golden Retrievers are a large breed and are considered senior after age 7. They should have an annual vet check, and it is especially important to check them regularly when you groom them for any lumps and bumps, weight gain or weight loss, or skin disease. Remember to keep nails short, and check that teeth are clean and not broken or diseased. Bad breath can be an indication of unhealthy teeth or, less commonly, disease. I highly recommend that all dogs over the age of 7 are put onto a natural joint supplement. As discussed earlier, most dogs do get arthritis, and many vets will recommend a joint supplement.

Charlotte

Like us, middle-aged dogs tend to gain weight, especially as their exercise tolerance levels decrease. Keep an eye on this and intervene sooner rather than later. It is important to keep your elderly dog lean, as this put less stress on old bones and joints. You will find that you need to feed them less as their metabolism slows and their exercise levels decrease. If their meals look too small, you can get creative and bulk up their meal with low-calorie additions like grated carrot, apple, and green beans so they do not feel hungry. They may also cope better with several small meals per day. Many diets are now made specifically for geriatric dogs, with added supplements to assist with age-related problems.

My next book will be on caring for the senior Golden, and will cover this topic in much more detail.

Saying Goodbye

I do not want to dwell on this stage of life too much, as this book is essentially about puppies, but the loss of a loved dog is something we all must deal with one day, and occasionally we must say goodbye to one of our beloved dogs earlier than expected. If and when your dog becomes seriously unwell, you may be faced with the difficult and heartbreaking decision of whether to euthanise your beloved companion. And the question of when is the right time can be even more daunting. It will be one of the hardest decisions you'll ever have to make, and if a younger dog is involved this grief can be even more overwhelming.

Decision-making guidelines

Speak with your veterinary team for support and guidance. Talk to your veterinarian about your dog's condition and prognosis and the likelihood of a return to normal life, or at least a new normal with good quality of life. Discuss all the treatment options available, and the pros and cons of each.

Here are a few steps you can take to help with this impossible decision:

- 🐾 **Complete a "quality-of-life scale".** We cannot ask our pets what their quality of life is like, so it's impossible to know exactly how they are feeling. Many vets use a quality-of-life scale that can provide you with objective information as to how your beloved pet's quality of life is likely to be progressing over time and in response to treatments. Dr. Alice Villalobos, DVM, developed such a scale, which is known as the HHHHHMM Scale. The five Hs stand for: Hurt, Hunger, Hydration, Hygiene, and Happiness. The two Ms stand for Mobility and More good days than bad. Patients are scored from 1–10, with 10 being ideal.

- 🐾 **Look at it from your dog's perspective.** What would your beloved pet want? You no doubt have a strong connection with your dog, and you want nothing but the best for them. If you are feeling unsure, take the time to think about what they would want you to do. Animals cannot speak, but many owners say that when they looked into their dog's eyes, they knew it was time.

- 🐾 **Speak to supportive friends and family.** Enlist your friends and family for support during this tough time. If your pet is part of the family, make the decision a shared one so that each member has a chance to discuss their thoughts and concerns and feel comfortable with the decision.

- 🐾 **Access animal bereavement counselling.** Contemplating losing a pet can feel just as difficult as losing a human family member, and some people really struggle to cope. You may have an overwhelming sense of guilt that interferes with your ability to look at the situation objectively. There are trained pet counsellors that can help you overcome your grief, and help you work through your feelings.

- 🐾 **Decide whether you would like your pet cremated or buried.** Today there are many options available. If you choose to get your pet cremated there are some beautiful urns that you can keep their ashes in. Cremation or burial is a deeply personal decision. If you're not sure, talk to your veterinary team about your options.

Poisonous Plants

🐾 Autumn Crocus	🐾 Golden Chain	🐾 Nightshade
🐾 Azaleas	🐾 Hyacinth	🐾 Oak Tree
🐾 Black Locust	🐾 Jack in the Pulpit	🐾 Oleander
🐾 Bleeding Heart	🐾 Jasmine	🐾 Rhododendron
🐾 Buttercups	🐾 Jimson Weed (Thorn Apple)	🐾 Rhubarb
🐾 Castor Bean	🐾 Lantana Camara (Red Sage)	🐾 Rosary Pea
🐾 Cherries (Wild and Cultivated)	🐾 Larkspur	🐾 Sago Palm
🐾 Daffodil	🐾 Laurels	🐾 Star of Bethlehem
🐾 Daphne	🐾 Lily of the Valley	🐾 Water Hemlock
🐾 Dieffenbachia (Dumb Cane)	🐾 Mayapple	
🐾 Elderberry	🐾 Mistletoe	
🐾 Elephant Ear	🐾 Monkshood	
🐾 Foxglove	🐾 Moonseed	
	🐾 Narcissus	

This list of toxic plants for dogs was gathered from the Cornell University <u>Department of Animal Science website</u>

Household Poisons

If you think your pet may have ingested a poison, always contact your vet for advice.

🐾 Alcohol	🐾 Chocolate (especially dark)	🐾 Macadamia nuts
🐾 Air fresheners	🐾 Coco mulch	🐾 Nicotine
🐾 Ant bait	🐾 Garden fertilisers	🐾 Onions
🐾 Anti-freeze	🐾 Grapes	🐾 Rat and mouse bait
🐾 Avocado	🐾 Human drugs (painkillers, ADHA, antidepressants, anticancer drugs)	🐾 Snail bait
🐾 Aromatherapy Oils		🐾 Xylitol (artificial sweetener)
🐾 Batteries	🐾 Heavy metals e.g. lead, zinc, mercury	
🐾 Caffeine		

Peanut butter and pumpkin biscuits

- 2 ½ cups whole wheat flour or oat flour
- 2 large eggs
- ½ cup mashed/canned pumpkin (or sweet potato)
- 2 tbsp peanut butter
- ½ tsp salt
- ½ tsp ground cinnamon

1. Preheat the oven to 350°F (175°C).

2. Combine flour, eggs, pumpkin, peanut butter, salt, and cinnamon in a bowl; stir with a spatula until combined.

3. Transfer mixture to a work surface and work it with your hands until mixture starts to come together. Add water a teaspoon at a time if needed to make the dough workable, but don't add too much; it should be dry and stiff.

4. Roll the dough to a thickness of ½ inch. Cut into ½-inch pieces and transfer to a baking sheet.

5. Bake in the preheated oven until dog treats are golden brown and crunchy, about 40 minutes. Let cool before serving to your dog.

Carrot and apple biscuits

- 1 ½ cups gluten-free flour
- ½ cup carrots, shredded
- ½ cup red apple, shredded
- 1 cup chicken or vegetable broth
- Cookie cutter

1. Preheat the oven to 400°F (200°C)
2. Squeeze excess moisture out of carrot and apple.
3. Fold together flour, carrots, apple, and chicken broth in a large mixing bowl.
4. Sprinkle countertop with about 1 tbsp flour and roll mixture flat to a thickness of about ½ inch using a rolling pin.
5. Using your favourite cookie cutter, cut biscuits until the mixture is used up.
6. Bake for 8–10 minutes or until lightly browned.

Cheese & bacon treats

- 1 ½ cups rolled oats.
- ½ cup shredded cheddar cheese
- 4 strips bacon, cooked and crumbled
- 2 eggs

1. Preheat oven to 350°F (180°C).
2. Add oats, cheese, and bacon to the bowl of a food processor and process until the mixture reaches a crumb-like consistency.
3. Add 2 eggs to food processor and process until mixture resembles a sticky dough.
4. Sprinkle flour or finely ground oats onto a wood cutting board and roll out dough to a thickness of about ¼ inch.
5. Using a cookie cutter, cut dough into desired shape.
6. Transfer dog treats to a parchment-lined baking sheet and cook for 20 minutes.
7. Cool treats completely and store in an airtight container.

Liver cake (good for training treats)

- 450 g (1 lb) raw beef or lamb liver
- 450 g (1 lb) self-rising flour (or gluten-free flour for dogs with allergies)
- 3 eggs
- 1 clove of garlic (or ½ teaspoon of minced garlic)
- Extra milk or water

1. Preheat oven to 350°F (180°C).
2. In a measuring bowl, crack the eggs and add milk or water to double the volume. Using a fork, mix well to blend.
3. Using a blender, liquefy the liver to a smooth consistency and add to egg mixture.
4. In a large bowl, combine with flour to make a sticky, dough-like consistency.
5. Transfer into baking tray(s). I personally separate into two batches and line my baking trays. You could be creative here and make a bone-shaped cake!
6. Bake for 45–60 minutes. Check on the cake at around 35 minutes – the top should be darkened and should bounce back when pressed lightly. These treats will last in the fridge for 2–3 days and in the freezer for up to 3 months.

Useful Websites

- National Golden Retriever Council Australia: www.ausngrc.org
- Golden Retriever Club, New Zealand: www.goldenretriever.org.nz
- Golden Retriever Club of America: www.grca.org
- The Golden Retriever Club UK: www.thegoldenretrieverclub.co.uk
- The Golden Retriever Breed Council UK: https://www.goldenretrieverbreedcouncil.co.uk/
- Golden Retriever Club of Scotland: http://www.goldenretrieverclubofscotland.com/
- Golden Retriever Club of Canada: www.grcc.net
- The Fédération Cynologique Internationale: http://www.fci.be/en/
- Dr. Dunbar's Dog Behaviour & Training Academy: https://www.dunbaracademy.com/
- Puppy Culture: https://shoppuppyculture.com/
- Susan Garrett's "Dogs That" https://dogsthat.com/
- ANKC breeders listing site (Australia): www.dogzonline.com.au
- Cooper and Kids (dogs and kids living safely): https://cooperandkids.com
- Kuranda dog beds: https://therian.com.au/product-category/kuranda-dog-cat-beds/
- Government site on dog poisons: http://agriculture.vic.gov.au/pets/dogs/dog-health/common-dog-poisons
- Fresh food feeding for dogs: https://www.facebook.com/groups/rawandfresh/

Recommended Reading

Some of these books may be out of print but can be purchased online secondhand.

Books on Golden Retrievers

- *Golden Retrievers* – Marilynn Morphet
- *The Ultimate Golden Retriever* – Valerie Foss
- *Golden Retrievers: An Owner's Companion* – Lyn Anderson
- *Golden Retrievers Today* – Valerie Foss
- *Golden Retrievers: An Owner's Guide* – Eric Allan
- *The New Complete Golden Retriever* – Gertrude Fischer

Books on dog health

- *The Dog Owner's Manual* – Karen Hedberg
- *Should I Spay or Neuter My Dog?* – Jane Lindquist
- *Caring For Your Dog* – Dr Bruce Fogle

Books on dog training

- *Before & After Getting Your Puppy* – Dr Ian Dunbar
- *Dog Training: The Gentle Modern Method* – David Weston
- *Easy Peasy Puppy Squeezy* – Steve Mann
- *When Pigs Fly* – Jane Killion
- *Canine Enrichment* – Shay Kelly
- *Think Dog: An Owner's Guide to Canine Psychology* – John Fisher
- *Don't Shoot the Dog: The New Art of Teaching and Training* – Karen Pryor
- *Clicker Training for Dogs* – Karen Pryor
- *The Other End of the Leash* – Patricia McConnell

ACKNOWLEDGEMENTS

Special thank you must go to Stephanie Ayres, Margot Stuckey and Chris Montgomery for their patience and editing, and to my son Tom who had to come home from overseas due to COVID and has been an amazing help with layout and production of my books.

Thank you to all those that have help contribute to this book, It is the culmination of many years' work, with advice from many people, including Mel Ritterman, (Cooper and Kids) Laura Mundy (behaviourist), Dr Karen Hedberg, Dr Robin Stanley (Animal Eye Care), Dr Roger Lavelle (Lavelle Diagnostic Imaging), Dr Richard Woolley (Cardiorespiratory Pet Referrals), the Australian National Kennel Council and National Golden Retriever Council of Australia, the Responsible Pet Ownership Education Program Victoria, and Virbac Animal Health.

Selected References

- 🐾 Sanborn, L J (2007). Long-term health risks and benefits associated with spay/neuter in dogs. National Animal Interest Alliance. Retrieved from <https://www.naiaonline.org/pdfs/LongTermHealthEffectsOfSpayNeuterInDogs.pdf>
- 🐾 Kustritz, MVR, Slater, MR, Weedon, GR, and Bushbyd, PA (2017). Determining optimal age for gonadectomy in the dog: A critical review of the literature to guide decision making. *Clinical Theriogenology*, 9(2). Retrieved from < https://www.fawavizslas.com/uploads/2/8/8/7/28870095/determining optimal age for gonadectomy in the dog clinical theriogenology 2017.pdf>
- 🐾 Dodge, E (1989). Critical periods in canine development. *Weimaraner Magazine*, October 1989.

Photo credits

Shutterstock-Yuriy Golub(front cover), Janelle Salvestrin, Brian Whipple (back cover), Lorraine Harrowfield, Dietmar Gregory, Carly Fitzgerald, Marni De Hoogd, Emma Jean Ford, Jenny McDonald, and Donna Ryan

Disclaimer

This guidebook has been written to provide helpful information on purchasing and raising a Golden Retriever. It is not meant to be used to diagnose or treat any medical conditions or serious behavioural problems. For diagnosis or treatment of any medical or behavioural condition, please consult a qualified veterinarian or animal behaviourist.

The author is not responsible for any specific conditions that may require medical supervision and is not liable for any damages or negative outcomes from any treatment, action application, or preparation to any animal or person reading or following the information in this book.

A litter of Camuka puppies bred by Jane

IMPORTANT DATES FOR YOUR PUPPY – RECORD CHART

PUPPY NAME _____ DATE OF BIRTH_____ GENDER M / F

BREEDER _____ MICROCHIP NUMBER_____

DATE	AGE	THINGS TO DO	TICK/RECORD	NOTES
	8 weeks	Worm puppy Vet check after puppy purchase Start puppy preschool Insure puppy Weigh puppy		*Your puppy should have had his first vaccination with the breeder and will require another 1 or 2 boosters depending on the vaccine used.*
	10 weeks	Vaccinate if due Weigh Worm Start to socialise your puppy		*Ask your vet about parasite prevention for heartworm, fleas, and ticks.* *Your puppy should now be attending puppy preschool.*
	12 weeks	Register puppy with local council Vaccinate if due Weigh Worm Start socialisation chart		***Worming** – your puppy needs to be wormed at 8, 10, and 12 weeks; then monthly until 6 months; then every 3 months for life.*
	4 months	Weigh Worm Vaccinate if due Start puppy training school		*Complete socialisation chart and continue with puppy school and training. Get puppy out and about seeing the world.*
	5 months	Worm Weigh		
	6 months	Worm Weigh		
	9 months	Worm Weigh		
	12–18 months	Worm Desex females (after first season) Vaccination booster due		
	12–24 months	Desex males Vaccination booster due		

Additional comments:

❧PUPPY SOCIALISATION CHART

Socialisation and training of a puppy is best done between the ages of 6 and 16 weeks. The goal of this chart is that the puppy will have positive experiences, not neutral or a bad one. It is important to watch your puppy's response and note what it is. Offer treats to help ensure the exposure is a success. Use this check list weekly and print a new one as required. **Tick each box as you do each task (4 times per week)**

More detail at www.drsophiayin.com

Gentle Handling	1	2	3	4
Check the eyes and ears				
Examine the mouth and teeth				
Hold feet, play with toes				
Trim toenails				
Holding puppy in your lap				
Putting on collar and lead or harness				
Wiping body with towel				
Brushing with soft brush				
Gentle restraint				

Unfamiliar People				
Women				
Tall men				
Men with beards				
Men in hats				
People wearing raincoats				
People with helmets				
People with masks				
Elderly				
People with walking frames, scooters				
Teenagers				
Varying nationality				
Toddlers (walking)				
Children playing				
Infants crawling				

Unfamiliar Dogs and animals				
Dogs who play well				
Other gentle puppies				
An older dog who may reprimand				
Cats				
Horses and livestock				
Poultry				
Other pets you may have				

New Surfaces				
Concrete				
Slippery floors				
Stones				
Wobbly surfaces				
Stairs				
Wet grass, puddles				
Frost, or snow				

Around The home				
Washing machine & dryer				
Vacuum cleaner				
Telephone				
Doorbell				
Dropped saucepans				
Lawn mower				
Whipper snipper				
Noisy tools				

Sounds	1	2	3	4
Thunder				
Fireworks				
Babies & children				
Alarms				
Dogs barking				
Doorbell				
Traffic				
Aeroplanes				
Sirens				
Hot air balloon				
Jack hammer				

Objects with wheels				
Garbage bins				
Cars				
Trucks				
Trains				
Trams				
Motor bike				
Mobile scooter				

Outside the home				
New neighborhood				
City streets				
High traffic streets				
Shopping Mall parking lot				
Inside buildings e.g. Bunnings				
Dog friendly events e.g. dog show				
Puppy training classes				
An unfamiliar house				

Objects				
Umbrella				
Brooms				
Balloons				
Flappy rubbish bag				
Traffic signs				
Metal pens or runs				
Metal surfaces				

Scan this code with your phone's camera for a printable PDF

Made in the USA
Monee, IL
09 December 2024

73069751R00048